Acclaim for Randall Kennedy

"[Kenn   illumi-
                                          and
nee-   uch
rancorou   uly
                                          sis

"Thoughtfu
   that [Kenn
   U.S. Suprem

"Fascinating. .

"[A] balanced a
   African-America

"Kennedy writes ve

"Kennedy provides re   ...cans to be
   considered black."   —*The New Times* (Miami)

"Kennedy, a scholar who can look with an unblemished lucidity
   at both sides of an argument, transcends what he acknowledges
   has become a personal issue for him to advance a debate for all
   of us."   arlotte)

Randall Kennedy

SELLOUT

Randall Kennedy is the Michael R. Klein Professor of Law at Harvard University. He is a member of the bars of the District of Columbia and the Supreme Court of the United States, a fellow of the American Academy of Arts and Sciences, and a member of the American Philosophical Association. His book *Race, Crime, and the Law* won the Robert F. Kennedy Book Award.

SELLOUT

SELLOUT

The Politics of Racial Betrayal

RANDALL KENNEDY

VINTAGE BOOKS
A Division of Random House, Inc.
New York

FIRST VINTAGE BOOKS EDITION, JANUARY 2009

The Library of Congress has cataloged the Pantheon edition as follows:
Kennedy, Randall.
Sellout : the politics of racial betrayal / Randall Kennedy.
p. cm.
Includes bibliographical references and index.
1. African Americans—Politics and government. 2. African American
politicians. 3. Thomas, Clarence. 4. Stereotypes (Social psychology)—
United States. 5. Stigma (Social Psychology)—United States.
6. Racism—United States. I. Title.
E185.615K377 2008
323.1196'073—dc22
2007028052

Vintage ISBN: 978-0-307-38842-1

Author photograph © C. J. Gunther
Book design by M. Kristen Bearse

www.vintagebooks.com

Printed in the United States of America
10 9 8 7 6 5 4 3 2 1

This book is dedicated to
Judge Henry Harold Kennedy, Jr.
Exemplary father, brother, son, husband, and friend

Contents

SELLOUT

PREFACE

"Do not be a slave to any form of selling out."

Oprah Winfrey, Commencement Address,
Howard University, May 2007

The specter of the "sellout" haunts the African-American imagination. A long-oppressed minority situated in the midst of a dominant white majority, blacks fear that whites will favor and corrupt acquiescent Negroes who, from positions of privilege, will neglect struggles for group elevation. African Americans fear that whites will empower "Oreos" who "look black but think white." African Americans fear that whites will promote black free riders and defectors who sap solidarity and discourage effective strategies for resisting subordination. Every social group—from the union to the organized crime family to the nation-state—confronts the challenge of exacting loyalty to the collective in the face of self-interest, hardship, or even danger.[1] That is why those engaged in the maintenance of groups expend considerable energy seeking to discover free-riding cheaters (think of the Internal Revenue Service in pursuit of tax evaders) or deceptive defectors (think of the Department of Justice in pursuit of traitors). If an entity as powerful as the United States of America periodically suffers from hysteria over perceived threats of internal subversion, it should be no surprise that African Americans—a marginalized, stigmatized, vulnerable racial minority—grapple with anxieties about racial betrayal.

A "sellout" is a person who betrays something to which she is said to owe allegiance.* When used in a racial context among African Americans, "sellout" is a disparaging term that refers to blacks who knowingly or with gross negligence act against the interest of blacks as a whole. Defining it that cleanly, however, offers a misleading sense of clarity. "Sellout" is a messy, volatile, contested term about which disagreement is rife, espe-

---

*For exploring words, *The Oxford English Dictionary* is an indispensible starting point. According to the OED, to "sell out" means "to betray a person or cause for gain." *The Oxford English Dictionary* (second edition, 1983, volume 14), p. 936.

Of course, like all words, "sellout" can have different meanings depending on the context in which it is used. A sellout performance is one in which all of the available seats at a venue are purchased or filled. Such popularity is often a positive signal of accomplishment. On the other hand, critics castigate as sellouts performers who are deemed to have compromised their artistry for the sake of popular approval that typically entails commercial advantage. The number of entertainers who have been accused of selling out is legion and includes such luminaries as Luciano Pavarotti, Bob Dylan, and Louis Armstrong.

In political struggles, those who compromise with adversaries often run the risk of being branded as sellouts. Examples include Michael Collins, Mohandas Gandhi, Anwar Sadat, and Yitzak Rabin—all of whom were assassinated.

cially when it comes to applying the label to specific persons or conduct.[2]

Sometimes "Uncle Tom" is used interchangeably with "sellout." In a *Washington Post* profile of Supreme Court Justice Clarence Thomas, two journalists write that "Uncle Tom is among the most searing insults a black American can hurl at a member of his own race."[3] They describe "Uncle Tom" as a "synonym for sellout, someone subservient to whites at the expense of his own people."[4] This usage is ironic. The original Uncle Tom—Harriet Beecher Stowe's Uncle Tom—was a character who chose death at the hand of his notorious owner, Simon Legree, rather than reveal the whereabouts of runaway slaves. Still, there are those who use "Uncle Tom" to refer to any black whose actions, in their view, retard African-American advancement. Others are more discriminating. For many of them, the label "sellout" is more damning than "Uncle Tom" or kindred epithets—"Aunt Thomasina," "Oreo," "snowflake," "handkerchief head," "white man's Negro," "Stepin Fetchit." While the latter insults refer to blacks who are deemed to be servile or otherwise lacking in an appropriate sense of racial pride or racial duty, "sellout" refers to someone who is dangerously antagonistic to blacks' well-being. He is worse than an enemy. An enemy is socially distant. The sellout, by contrast, is (or is thought to be) a member of the family, tribe, nation, or race. The sellout is a person who is trusted because of his perceived membership in a given group—trusted until he shows his "true colors," by which time he has often done harm to those who viewed him as a kinsman or fellow citizen.

Reputable people use "sellout" as an insult, and it is broadly seen as serving a useful purpose by identifying and stigmatizing a real menace: the black race traitor. Thus, a person accused of being a sellout will typically want to refute the charge, since, if it is believed, the indictment will generate all manner of negative consequences, including ostracism or even reprisal.

Suspicions of racial betrayal in black America have a long history. The extraordinary Martin R. Delany, whom some have dubbed the "father of black nationalism," was fired upon by black militiamen who denounced him as a traitor when, in the 1870s, he rejected the Republican Party, allied himself with the Democrats, and campaigned for a former Confederate general and opponent of Reconstruction.[5]* Frederick Douglass, the preeminent black abolitionist, was excoriated by many African Americans as a turncoat when he married a white woman.† Angered by W. E. B. DuBois's disapproval of black protest after the American entry into World War I, black dissidents contemptuously labeled as a Benedict Arnold‡ the most outstanding activist-intellectual in black American history.§

---

*See pages 37–38.
†See page 63.
‡Benedict Arnold (1741–1801) was a general who initially fought for the American colonies in the Revolutionary War but then betrayed them by scheming to surrender a key fort to the British. See Willard Sterne Randall, *Benedict Arnold: Patriot and Traitor* (1990). Benedict Arnold's name has become synonymous with treachery, just as Clarence Thomas's name is now becoming synonymous with selling out. See page 88.
§See pages 47–48.

Suspicions regarding racial betrayal continue to be omnipresent. From the outset of his historic presidential campaign, Barack Obama has had to deal with doubts about his loyalty to blackness because of his ancestry (his mother was white), his upbringing (he was raised in Hawaii, apart from a cohesive black community), and perhaps most of all because many white people have strongly supported him. Discussing Obama, journalist Peter Beinart rightly noted that "being the 'good' black is tricky. The more whites love you, the more you must reassure your own community that you are still one of them. And the more you do that, the more you jeopardize your white support."[6] Obama himself addressed the issue squarely in a speech to the National Association of Black Journalists. Many blacks, he observed, remain ensnared by the notion that "if you appeal to white folks, there must be something wrong."[7]

Questions regarding racial loyalty also dog Condoleezza Rice, Clarence Thomas, Vernon Jordan, Colin Powell, and the list goes on. Indeed, with the possible exception of athletes, blacks who attain success in a multiracial setting will always sooner or later encounter whispered insinuations or shouted allegations that their achievement is attributable, at least in part, to "selling out." "Middle-class black folk," journalist Jill Nelson observes, "tend to grow up feeling we have something to prove—not just to white folks, but to just about everyone, including each other. We greet one another with skepticism, treating each other as potential Eurocentric sellouts ... until proven otherwise."[8] Many

Negroes* are delighted when other blacks "make it" in their chosen field of endeavor; they see breakthroughs for one as advances for all. But for some, the very fact of success, especially when it stems substantially from white support, is reason enough to question an African American's racial bona fides. Why, they ask, do the white folks

---

*Throughout this book I use as synonyms "black," "Negro," "colored," "Afro-American," "African American," and "people of color." I realize that vigorous political struggles have shaped the history of these terms and that today some of them—e.g., "Negro" and "colored"—are seen as either antiquated or insulting. In my view, words take their meaning from the context in which they are used. A large part of the context is the aim of the speaker or writer. My aim is to convey respectfulness in using all of these terms. My practice stems largely from sentiment. I got in the habit of using "Negro" when I served as a law clerk to Justice Thurgood Marshall in 1983–1984. He preferred that term and directed his clerks to use it (though at the end of his tenure Justice Marshall began to use "Afro-American" as a substitute for "Negro"). Using "Negro" reminds me of the great justice and provides a small but personally meaningful way for me to pay homage to him. "Negro" has been harshly criticized. See, for example, Richard B. Moore, *The Name "Negro": Its Origin and Evil Use* (1960). It has also been stoutly defended, however. See W. E. B. DuBois, *Writings* (Library of America College Editions, Nathan Huggins, ed., 1996), p. 1219 ("'Negro' is a fine word").

"Colored," too, has been criticized. See *The Associated Press Stylebook* 52 (2004) ("Colored . . . is considered derogatory and should not be used"). But my formidable grandmother Lillian Veta Spann used "colored," and that term remains part of the title of one of the great black uplift organizations in the United States: the NAACP, the National Association for the Advancement of Colored People. I am pleased by the company I keep with respect to racial nomenclature. Good enough for Thurgood Marshall, Lillian Veta Spann, W. E. B. DuBois, and the NAACP, "Negro" and "colored" are good enough for me.

permit this Negro to succeed? He must, they conclude, be collaborating.

In the pages that follow I describe the contours of African-American anxiety over racial betrayal. I follow this angst in the writings of black activists and intellectuals and chronicle episodes of alleged racial treachery. I show how allegations of selling out are currently triggered by a wide range of actions—marrying a white person, passing, "acting white," "speaking white," "thinking white," describing oneself as "multiracial," living in a white neighborhood, serving as a police officer or a prosecutor, working as an attorney for an elite law firm, opposing affirmative action. I delineate the negative effects that attend allegations of racial treachery: the truncation of needed debate, the resentment of those who feel intimidated by monitors of black political correctness, the nourishing of demagogues whose "leadership" consists largely of impugning the racial authenticity of rivals. I differ, however, with those who maintain that in light of these side effects the concept of racial betrayal should be repudiated wholesale. This approach neglects the requirement for maintaining any community—policing the group's boundaries—and the benefits of appropriate ostracism (the suppression of feelings, ideas, and conduct that ought to be suppressed). If there is going to exist an imagined community known as Black America, there must also exist some point at which a citizen of Black America can rightly be charged with having done something that betrays that polity. But because Black America is wildly heterogeneous, because determining what is in the best interest of diverse communities is almost always controversial, and because black Americans ought to have wide latitude in expressing themselves, extreme care should attend the making of any such allegations. All too often, in framing their indictments, prosecutors of "sellouts" display alarming sloppiness. I call for more care. I urge that indictments for racial betrayal be drawn more cautiously and taken more seriously. Those originating such charges should be held accountable if allegations are found wanting. Errant accusers should be made to feel the pain of ostracism just as their targets do.

Before addressing further the idea of racial betrayal in Black America, however, I should attend more closely to distinguishing "blacks" from "nonblacks." To betray a polity one must be a member of it. A person may be an enemy of a group to which he is an outsider. But to *betray* a group, he must be an insider. To explore, then, the idea of the sellout in Black America, I begin with a question: Who is "black"?

One

Who Is "Black"?

"How difficult it sometimes is to know where the black begins and the white ends."

Booker T. Washington, *Up from Slavery* (1901)

Soon after declaring his candidacy for the presidency of the United States, Senator Barack Obama was asked on the television program *60 Minutes* when he had "decided" that he was black.[1] One of the reasons the interviewer posed this question is that Obama's mother was a white American and his father a black Kenyan. Obama, moreover, had had little contact with his father; he was raised mainly in Hawaii by his mother and her relatives, in settings far afield from conventional black American communities.[2] Against this backdrop, some observers have questioned Obama's racial standing. "Obama isn't black," the journalist Debra J. Dickerson asserts, because "in our political and social reality [black] means those descended from West African slaves." Rather, Dickerson continues, "by virtue of his white American mom and his Kenyan dad . . . [Obama] is an American of African immigrant extraction."[3]*

Obama responded to the question on *60 Minutes* by distancing himself from the idea that he had "decided" to be black. He focused on three other considerations: his appearance, the response of onlookers to his appearance, and his shared experience of those responses with others also perceived to be "black." "[I]f you look African American in this society," he remarked, "you're treated as an African American."[4] In 1940, W. E. B. DuBois quipped that "the black man is a person who must ride 'Jim Crow' in Georgia."[5] Obama updated that view, noting that when he tried to catch taxis, drivers were not confused about his race; they all too often refused to pick him up for racially discriminatory reasons, just as they all too often sped by other "black" men.

Discussion of Obama's racial identity is a highly publicized instance of a feature of American race relations that is often ignored or misunderstood though it has deep historical roots. Many people believe that determining who is "black" is rather easy, a task simplified by the administration of the one-drop rule.[6] Under the one-drop

---

*Dickerson's widely noted article was not a critique of Obama; it was a skeptical assessment of white people's support for him. Whites, she complained, "are engaged in a paroxysm of self-congratulation." She maintained that if Obama were a black man born of native-born African Americans, whites would find it more difficult to embrace him. According to Dickerson, "If [Obama] were Ronald Washington from Detroit, even with the same résumé, he wouldn't be getting this kind of love." See "Colorblind," Salon.com, Jan. 22, 2007.

rule, any discernible African ancestry stamps a person as "black." A principal purpose of this doctrine was to address "the problem" of children born of interracial sex who would bear a mixture of physical markers inherited from ancestors situated on different sides of the race line. White supremacists hoped that by definitively categorizing as "African," "black," "Negro," or "colored" anyone whose appearance signaled the presence of an African ancestor, the one-drop rule would protect white bloodlines. It mirrored and stoked Negrophobia by proclaiming that even the tiniest dab of Negro ancestry was sufficiently contaminating to make a person a "nigger." Many white racists have believed what a character exclaims in Thomas Dixon's novel *The Leopard's Spots*—that "a single drop" of Negro blood "kinks the hair, flattens the nose, thickens the lip, puts out the light of intellect, and lights the fires of brutal passions."[7]*

Many champions of black advancement, however, have also become devotees of the one-drop rule (bereft, of course, of its white supremacist intentions). In her

---

*Many artists have created drama out of the one-drop rule. Satirizing it, Mark Twain has one of his characters explain why a person who looks white and has mostly white ancestors is nonetheless considered "black"—"Thirty-one thirty-seconds of you is white and one thirty-second is nigger, and that part of you is your soul." See Mark Twain, *Pudd'nhead Wilson and Those Extraordinary Twins* (1894; reprint 1980). Playing off of the one-drop rule in her novel *Show Boat* (1926), Edna Ferber portrays Steve, a white man, who marries Julie, a Negro passing for white. Informed that the couple are in violation of a state antimiscegenation statute, a Mississippi sheriff moves to take them into custody. Desperate to avoid arrest, Steve pricks Julie's

richly detailed defense of the doctrine, Professor Christine B. Hickman writes:

> The Devil fashioned [the one-drop rule] out of racism, malice, greed, lust and ignorance, but in so doing he also accomplished good: His rule created the African-American race as we know it today, and while this race had its origins in the peoples of three continents and its members can look very different from one another, over the centuries the Devil's one-drop rule united this race as a people in the fight against slavery, segregation and racial injustice.[8]

The one-drop rule helped to funnel into one racial camp people who might otherwise have been splintered. It is because of the one-drop rule that some of the most significant leaders among African Americans are considered "black" or "Negro" despite their "white" ancestry; here I think immediately of Frederick Douglass and W. E. B. DuBois. Long denounced as a method for protecting whites against the taint of Negro blood, the one-drop rule is now embraced by some devotees of black unity as a way of reinforcing solidarity and discouraging exit by "blacks" who might otherwise prefer to reinvent themselves racially.

Despite its evident significance, however, the one-drop rule has never been an unchallenged guide to racial

---

finger and sucks some of her blood. When the sheriff approaches, Steve says, "You wouldn't call a man a white man that's got negro blood in him, would you?" "No, I wouldn't; not in Mississippi," the sheriff replies. "One drop of nigger blood makes you a nigger in these parts." That formulation allows the pair to remain free.

definition.* For a long period, several states formally defined as "white" individuals with known "black" ancestors. Until early in the twentieth century, several states, including Florida, Georgia, and South Carolina, statutorily decreed that an individual was considered white so long as he or she did not have more than one-eighth Negro "blood." In Virginia, until 1910, a person could be deemed white as long as he or she did not have more than twenty-four percent Negro blood. Not until 1924 did the Old Dominion adopt the one-drop rule.[9] True, in many places, the mere appearance of being a Negro was sufficient to trigger mistreatment, regardless of one's genealogy or the words of some arcane statute purporting to define racial status. Still, the assigning of racial identity by white authorities has occasioned far more controversy than is generally realized.

*A sufficiently stringent interpretation of the one-drop rule could turn the United States into a majority "black" nation. If humankind's origins are located in Africa, as many scientists now contend, *all* humans may be carrying a genetic legacy from the so-called Dark Continent. See, e.g., Chris Stringer and Peter Andrews, *The Complete World of Human Evolution* (2005); Roger Lewin, *Human Evolution: An Illustrated Introduction* (fifth edition, 2005). It is also very likely, given the nature of interracial sexual intermingling in colonial and antebellum North America, that there are millions of people who think of themselves as "white" and are perceived socially to be "white," but who have an unknown American-born black ancestor— the proverbial "nigger in the woodpile." See Randall Kennedy, *Interracial Intimacies: Sex, Marriage, Identity, and Adoption* (2003), and Robert P. Stuckert, "African Ancestry of the White American Population," 58 *Ohio Journal of Science* 155 (1958). Also Kwame Anthony Appiah, "Does Truth Matter to Identity?" in *Race or Ethnicity? On Black and Latino Identity,* Jorge J. E. Gracia, ed. (2007), pp. 34–35.

Just as some "whites" have adopted rules of racial identification at variance with the one-drop rule, so, too, have some "blacks." Light-skinned descendants of interracial unions have at various times attempted to set themselves apart from those with darker hues. They have labeled themselves differently, for example, eschewing "black" or "Negro" in favor of "FMC"—"free men of color"—or similar formulations. They have created social organizations that resolutely excluded those deemed to be "too dark"—those darker than a light-brown paper bag or those in whose wrists one cannot discern blue veins.[10] They have insisted upon marrying people who were as light as, or preferably lighter than, themselves. The one-drop rule lumps all "colored" people together regardless of the extent to which they are partially white in appearance or ancestry. But some light-skinned people of color have rejected that formula and insisted upon distinguishing themselves from "real" Negroes.* Consider the case of William Ellison, who was born into slavery in 1790 in South Carolina. Allowed to purchase his freedom (by a white man who may well have been his biological father), Ellison amassed a sizable fortune, bought and sold slaves, contributed funds to pro-

---

When white racial purists sought to amend Virginia's Racial Integrity Act to make its racial distinctions even more discriminatory, white legislators balked, recognizing that a further narrowing of definitions of whiteness would lead to a situation in which there would be few "white" Virginians left. See Richard B. Sherman, "'The Last Stand': The Fight for Racial Integrity in Virginia in the 1920s," 54 *Journal of Southern History* 1 (1988).

*Now it is commonplace for African Americans to refer to themselves as black. Prior to the late 1960s, however, many Negroes

slavery vigilantes, aided the Confederacy, and then, after the Civil War, supported the opponents of Reconstruction. Today many people would describe Ellison as "black" despite his obvious multiraciality. Yet Ellison "did not consider himself a black man but a man of color, a mulatto, a man neither black nor white, a brown man."[11]

Between 1850 and 1920, the United States Census demarcated a category for the "mulatto." Enumerators were initially given virtually no guidance;[12] they used their own judgment, mainly based on appearance, to determine who was "black" as opposed to "mulatto." In 1870, census officials noted that the "mulatto" category included "quadroons, octoroons and all persons having any perceptible trace of African blood."[13] In 1890, officials supplemented the "white," "black," and "mulatto" categories with two new classifications that had previously been subsumed within the definition for mulatto. They admonished enumerators to

> [b]e particularly careful to distinguish between blacks, mulattoes, quadroons, and octoroons. The word "black"

------

perceived it as an insult to be called black. A central achievement of the Black Power Movement was to remove, at least from Negroes' minds, much of the stigma that America's white supremacist culture had heaped upon "black." An important artifact of that movement was the anthem by Soul Brother Number One, James Brown, "Say It Loud, I'm Black and I'm Proud." The very need to insist upon that proposition, however, was indicative of the devalued status that had befallen blackness and that continues to burden it in American culture. See Kathy Russell, Midge Wilson, and Ronald Hall, *The Color Complex: The Politics of Skin Color Among African Americans* (1992); Trina Jones, "Shades of Brown: The Law of Skin Color," 49 *Duke Law Journal* 1487 (2000).

should be used to describe those persons who have three-fourths or more black blood; "mulatto," those persons who have three-eighths to five-eighths black blood; "quadroon," those persons who have one-fourth black blood; and "octoroon," those persons who have one-eighth or any trace of black blood.[14]

At no point were enumerators provided with a methodology for extracting this information or discerning these differences.

The idea of the mulatto has been a gathering point for a wide variety of racial prejudices, fears, myths, and speculations.[15] For one thing, throughout American history there has been a tendency on the part of whites and blacks to favor mulattoes and other mixed-race colored people over plain "blacks." This tendency has been fueled, in large part, by the logic of white supremacy: since whiteness has been perceived to be superior to blackness, lighter complexions have been accorded more prestige than darker ones. Hence the saying: "If you're black, go back; if you're brown, stick around; if you're white, you're alright."[16]*

The baleful efflorescence of racist sentiments in the post–World War I era prompted the Census Bureau to simplify its stratification of the American pigmentocracy. After 1920, the Bureau ceased enumerating mulattoes. It adopted the one-drop rule, declaring that persons of

---

*Some raceologists, however, have posited that mulattoes are inferior to both "pure" whites and "pure" blacks. Defenders of

"mixed blood" would be "classified according to the nonwhite racial strain . . . [A person] of mixed white . . . and Negro . . . is classified as . . . a Negro . . . regardless of the amount of white blood [he carries]."[17] Under the new regime, writes Professor Joel Williamson, "all Negroes did look alike. On the one side, there were simply Negroes, and on the other the melting pot was busy making everyone [else, except Asians] simply white. Obviously the Bureau was quite willing to add its strength to the effort to create a simply biracial America."[18]

Although skin color is undoubtedly the most salient signal of racial identity in America, other actual or imagined bodily features have also been seen as distinctive markers of Negritude. These include the shapes of heads, feet, lips, and noses as well as the texture of hair.[19] Adjudicating the race of plaintiffs suing for their freedom, a Virginia judge asserted in 1806 that:

> Nature has stamped upon the African and his descendants two characteristic marks, besides the difference of complexion, which often remain visible long after the characteristic distinction of color either disappears or becomes doubtful; a flat nose and a wooly head of hair. The latter of these characteristics disappears the last of all; and so strong an ingredient in the African constitution is this latter char-

---

antimiscegenation laws pointed to the alleged inferiority of mulattoes as a basis for prohibiting interracial marriage. See Robert Brent Toplin, "Between Black and White: Attitudes Toward Southern Mulattoes, 1830–1861," 45 *Journal of Southern History* 185 (1979), and *Perez v. Lippold,* 198 P.2d 17 (1948) (Shenk, J., dissenting).

acter, that it predominates uniformly where the party is in equal degree descended from parents of different complexions.[20]

Yet, the very words used as labels for races—"white," "black," "red," "yellow," and "brown"—highlight the centrality of complexion in American racial consciousness. Skin color has long been the main physiological feature of the uniform that is widely seen as racially identifying the wearer.

So long as procreation stems from parents of the same race, appearance and lineage are typically congruent. Interracial unions give rise to added complexity. Interracial amalgamation will produce some individuals whose features diverge from those commonly ascribed to the races of their ancestors. When conflict arises between looks and lineage, it is the former that usually emerges as the more influential of the two. As Professor Robert Westley observes, "no one who is visually apprehended as Black . . . turns out to be white. . . . The judgment of Blackness is fixed, immediate, irreversible."[21] In notable instances whites have been willing to grant what Professor Daniel Sharfstein terms "racial amnesty" to individuals who appeared to be white.[22] The key to such amnesty, however, has been the appearance of the individuals in question; if they looked obviously "colored" there has been no controversy. They are labeled "colored" or "black" or "Negro" and that is the end of it. Only if they possessed physical traits that might lead them to be seen as white (or something else nonblack) would space be opened allowing for wiggle room in determining their racial placement.

Consider the early nineteenth-century North Carolina case *Gobu v. Gobu*,[23] in which a white girl found an abandoned baby whom she claimed as her slave. When this enslaved boy grew to maturity he sued for his freedom. No one knew the identity of his biological parents. In appearance, according to the court, he was "of an olive colour, between black and yellow, had long hair and a prominent nose." Judge John Louis Taylor expressly states that if he had recognized the plaintiff as "black," the plaintiff would have borne the burden of proving that he was not a slave. In Judge Taylor's words: "I acquiesce in the . . . presumption of every black person being a slave." But the plaintiff was not "black"; he was of "mixed blood," meaning that his mother might have been white or an Indian.* Given these possibilities, and the absence of any other pertinent evidence, the judge required the slaveholder to bear the burden of proving that the plaintiff was properly enslaved. The judge decided, in short, to give the plaintiff the benefit of

---

*In North Carolina, as in all antebellum slave states, a child inherited the status of his or her mother. If the mother was free, regardless of her race, the child was free. Race played an important role in determining one's status in that blacks were presumed to be enslaved while whites were presumed to be free. Some individuals who were "white" as defined by state laws were nonetheless slaves because their mothers were slaves. In some jurisdictions in the colonial period, white women who married enslaved black men were themselves reduced to slavery, a status that their children would then inherit. See Thomas

the doubt—a benefit withheld from anyone deemed by appearance to be "black."

Neither appearance nor lineage nor the concatenation of the two exhaust the menu of ingredients that have figured into determinations of race. Consider the lawsuit in South Carolina in 1940 in which Virginia Bennett challenged the will of her deceased father, Franklin Capers Bennett.[24] While leaving Virginia unmentioned, the will bequeathed Franklin's entire estate to his second wife, Louetta Chassereau Bennett. Virginia attacked the validity of Louetta's marriage to Franklin, asserting among other things that the union had violated the state's antimiscegenation law. According to Virginia, Louetta was colored, inasmuch as she was more than one-eighth Negro, and was thus prohibited from marrying Franklin, a white man. Virginia's motivation was clear. She wanted to obtain portions of Franklin's estate that would be lost to her if her father's marriage to Louetta was upheld.*

The Supreme Court of South Carolina rejected Virginia's challenge. It ruled that Louetta was not a Negro, despite the presence of "some Negro blood in her veins," because she possessed a reputation as a white person—in the court's words, she had been "generally accepted as

---

D. Morris, *Southern Slavery and the Law, 1619–1860* (1996), and Randall Kennedy, *Interracial Intimacies: Sex, Marriage, Identity, and Adoption* (2003).

*Under South Carolina state law, an individual could will no more than one-quarter of his or her estate to anyone other than a spouse. If it could be established that the marriage had been invalid, it would follow that only one-fourth of Franklin Bennett's estate could pass to the woman he had believed was his wife. The remaining

white"—and because she had long "acted white," by doing such things as marrying a white man, attending a white church, sending her children to white schools, and voting in political primaries open only to whites.*

The ruling in favor of Louetta Bennett, despite her "negro blood," was firmly rooted in precedent. As far back as 1835, the South Carolina judiciary had weighed considerations other than complexion and lineage in determining racial identification. "We cannot say what admixture of negro blood will make a colored person," Judge William Harper declared. "The condition of the individual is not to be determined solely by a distinct and visible mixture of negro blood, but by reputation, by his reception into society, and [by] his having commonly experienced the privileges of a white man."[25]

In the process by which individuals are racialized, they

---

three-quarters would then devolve to relatives, with Virginia presumably standing first in line to benefit. *Bennett v. Bennett,* 10 S.E.2d 23 (1940).

*To the trial judge it was significant that

> upon the death of [Louetta's] father and mother, she was first taken into the home of white people; then she was placed in a church orphanage for white children; she was confirmed . . . as a communicant of the Holy Communion Church of Charleston, a white church; she was taken from the orphanage and placed in a white home as a member of the family; she married a white man, the marriage was solemnized [in] a white church; she votes in the democratic primaries, both City and State, whose rules bar negroes from voting; her children attend the white public schools . . . ; she is generally accepted as a white person.

Bennett v. Bennett, 10 S.E.2d 23, 33 (1940).

have little or no control over certain factors—the color of their skin, the identity of their ancestors, the judgments of others, the ascendant protocols of racial categorization. Barack Obama, for instance, has no control over one of the most significant aspects of his case: the fact that some American-born Negroes decline to acknowledge as "African American" or "black" African-born Negroes or their progeny.* Professor Valerie Smith notes that "Obama's 'black credentials' have been questioned as much because of his Kenyan father as his white mother."[26] Those who have raised questions on this score emphasize the centrality of slavery in America to their definition of "blackness": to them, a "black" must have an ancestral tie to enslavement in America—clearly a circumstance over which an individual today has no control.

Within constraints of varying degrees, however, individuals can and do exercise choice in determining racial identity. Some people who would be widely accepted bearing any one of several racial labels insist upon describing themselves monoracially as black.[27] Others insist upon describing themselves as "multiracial."[28] Some people resolutely refuse to identify themselves racially at all,

---

* "African American" is often used synonymously with "black." But white and black Africans who have migrated to the United States have caused consternation in some quarters by designating themselves "African Americans." There are some who contend that the appellation "African American" should be reserved exclusively for American-born blacks. See Rachel L. Swarns, "'African-American' Becomes a Term for Debate," *New York Times*, Aug. 29, 2004.

believing the very concept of race to be a mischievous delusion. Ask them to assign themselves to a race and they reply "the human race." The golfer Tiger Woods, declining to identify himself simply as "black," famously coined the term "Cablinasian" (Caucasian, Black, Indian, and Asian) to identify himself racially.[29]* In the 2000 census, the federal government allowed individuals to assign themselves to one or more of six racial categories.[†]

Another manifestation of choice in racial determination arises from "passing": holding oneself out in a fashion that enables the adoption of specific roles or identities from which one would otherwise be barred by prevailing social standards. The classic racial passer in the United States is the "White Negro," an individual whose physical appearance allows him to present himself as "white" but whose "black" lineage (if publicized) would make him a Negro according to ascendant racial rules. More will be said later about the White Negro inasmuch as the black who migrates into whiteness is often seen as a race traitor.[‡] For now I will focus on the

---

*In the 2000 census, 10,672 persons identified themselves racially as White, Black, Indian, and Asian. See Table 2, Population of Two or More Races, Including All Combinations, for the United States: 2000, in Elizabeth M. Grieco and Rachel C. Cassidy, *Overview of Race and Hispanic Origin 2000* (2001) (U.S. Census Bureau).

†The six were: "White," "Black or African American," "American Indian and Alaska Native," "Asian," "Native Hawaiian and Other Pacific Islander," and "Some Other Race." The overwhelming majority of Americans, nearly 98 percent, identified themselves by reference to only one race. See Grieco and Cassidy, *Overview of Race.*

‡See pages 144–185.

"Black Caucasian," the person who holds himself out as black though according to dominant racial protocols he is "really" white. One such person was Mark L. Stebbins.[30] Stebbins's parents are identified as white on his birth certificate. He has blue eyes (though his brown hair is reportedly "tightly curled" and his nose is "broad"). He says that until his twenties he thought of himself as white. Over time, however, Stebbins attained a "gradual realization" that he was black. He led civil-rights demonstrations in the 1960s, married a black woman (a previous wife had been white), and in the '80s succeeded in winning a seat on the Stockton, California, city council. He held himself out as a black candidate in a jurisdiction in which blacks constituted 37 percent of the electorate, Latinos 46 percent, and whites and others the remaining portion.

The man whom Stebbins unseated, Ralph L. White, was a black man who later attempted to regain his position pursuant to an electoral recall of Stebbins. White argued that voters should recall Stebbins because he had lied to them in holding himself out as black. White based the charges on what he had learned from Stebbins's birth certificate: that his rival's parents were listed as "white." According to Stebbins's antagonist: "If the momma is an elephant and the daddy is an elephant, they durn sure can't have no lion."[31] In other words, if Stebbins's parents were white he could not possibly be black.*

---

*Of course, the concept of "parent" brings still other neglected issues into play. Legal parentage and biological parentage often

Stebbins insisted that he was black, despite the revelations of his birth certificate, and succeeded in attracting the support of some blacks who accepted his self-identification. Noting the continuing "curse" associated with blackness in America, one supporter voiced the proposition that if Stebbins was willing to publicly embrace this stigmatized identity then he should be permitted to do so. Another supporter who accepted Stebbins's self-definition mentioned that the embattled councilman "thinks black."[32]

Although Stebbins successfully weathered the initial recall vote, he eventually succumbed. "Nine months after having been voted out in the regular election, White was reinstated as councilman and Stebbins expelled from office—presumably for having committed 'racial' fraud."[33]

Soon after Stebbins's ordeal, two brothers in Massachusetts encountered a government bureaucracy that rejected their attempts to gain official recognition as blacks.[34] Seeking jobs as firefighters in Boston in 1975, Paul and Philip Malone identified themselves on their applications as "white." They were unsuccessful. Two years later they reapplied, but this time indicated that they were black—a "fact" that undoubtedly improved

---

overlap but may diverge. A person's legal parents may be of one race but his biological parents—perhaps his *secretly* biological parents— may be of another race. In some of the newspaper accounts of Stebbins's experience, there is an insinuation that a close male biological ancestor may have been black and the genetic source of his frizzy hair and broad nose.

their chances of being selected, since the fire department was operating under a court-ordered affirmative-action plan intended to remedy a long history of antiblack racial exclusion. The Malones succeeded on their second try. A decade later, when one of the brothers pursued a promotion, someone told fire department officials that both were racial impostors. In their defense, the Malones insisted that they were black, maintaining that after their initial rejection by the fire department, they had discovered that their maternal great-grandmother had been a Negro. The personnel administrator for the Commonwealth of Massachusetts invited the Malones to support their claim by reference to visual observation of their features, documentary evidence establishing black ancestry, or evidence that they or their families held themselves out to be black and are considered to be black. The administrator further stipulated that the Malones would be entitled to a favorable ruling even in the absence of such evidence if they could show that they had acted in good faith.

An internal hearing gave the Malones an opportunity to make their case. The officer presiding noted that the brothers did not appear to be black and that there existed no convincing documentary evidence linking them to even any remote black ancestry. "White" was the racial designation stamped on the birth certificates of both men, of their parents, and of their parents' parents. As for the maternal great-grandmother whom the Malone brothers described as being black, the hearing officer dismissed their photograph of her as inconclusive. Finally, the officer found no evidence that the Malones had ever identified themselves as black except in their attempt to benefit from the fire department's affirmative-action program. Against this backdrop, the personnel administrator concluded, in a ruling upheld judicially, that the Malones failed to meet either an "objective" standard of blackness (based on appearance, lineage, or reputation) or a "subjective" standard of blackness (based on whether in good faith they considered themselves to be black when they applied for their positions as African-American candidates).

I return now to the question with which I began: "Who is 'black'?" The answer is uncertain.* Much depends on the decision-maker at hand, as opinions vary widely. Appearance has been the single most influential criterion; dark skin has typically been a decisive indicator foreclosing

---

*It might seem odd that at this late date the criteria for membership in Black America is uncertain. Recall, though, the vexing period of uncertainty regarding the criteria for United States citizenship. As with so many key questions regarding American society, race relations lay at the center of the controversy. In the infamous case of *Dred Scott v. Sanford,* 60 U.S. 393 (1856), the Supreme Court held that regardless of status as slaves or free persons, blacks were ineligible for United States citizenship. Citizenship through birthright was conclusively settled only in 1868 by the ratification of the Fourteenth Amendment to the United States Constitution. See Randall Kennedy, "Dred Scott and African American Citizenship," in *Diversity and Citizenship: Rediscovering American Nationhood,* Gary Jacobsohn and Susan Dunn, eds. (1996).

controversy. But in the modern era of self-identification, even that formerly secure standard wobbles. While appearance is often decisive in social interactions, in the United States today virtually anyone can be "black" without fear of legal sanction so long as the person can persuasively show that he or she sincerely considers himself or herself to be black.

Barack Obama has suggested that there has been little or no choice on his part in affixing his racial identity. In saying this he is correct in a certain way but erroneous in another. He is correct in suggesting that for most American onlookers his appearance itself proclaims him to be black. He is erroneous, however, in suggesting that his own choices have played little or no part in making him black. After all, despite his appearance, he could have done what Tiger Woods and many other multiracial Americans have done—opted for a designation other than "black" or "African American."* That he refrained from doing so was not a foregone conclusion, but instead a decision of the sort that his inquisitor on *60 Minutes* was widely criticized for seeking to explore. Obama's choice to label himself "black," moreover, is reinforced by additional congruent decisions—the choice to be a

---

*Many detractors have accused Woods of being "in denial" that he is widely seen as black. Hence, one hears ridiculing statements such as: "Wait until he is stopped by a racist cop one night. *Then* he'll discover that he's black!" Woods, however, did not deny that many people perceive him as "black." His point was that their perception should not be conclusive in defining him, that he had something to say about the racial label he would wear. See Eammon Callan, "The Ethics of Assimilation," *Ethics* 115 (April 2005), p. 482, n. 16.

congregant in a predominantly black church, the choice to reside in a predominantly black neighborhood, the choice to marry a black woman.

Why, one wonders, did Obama insistently play down the matter of choice? While there are a range of possible explanations, one is especially pertinent to the study of Black American anxiety over racial betrayal. Perhaps Obama wanted to convey the message that his connection to blackness is indissoluble, rooted in something beyond his control and thus beyond withdrawal. To have said that at some point he "decided" to be black, Obama would have immediately distanced himself from the majority of African Americans who do not perceive themselves as having the option to make such a decision. To be able to choose to be black brings with it the possibility of changing one's mind in the future—a prospect of potential abandonment that many African Americans find quite disturbing.

Two

The Idea of the Sellout in Black American History

"Every people has its share of opportunists, profiteers, free-loaders, and escapists."

Martin Luther King, Jr., "The Sword That Heals,"
The Critic, June–July 1964

Why did leading champions of black uplift and communal resistance voice anxiety about racial betrayal during the first two centuries of United States history? What notable episodes of apparent racial treachery stoked those worries? Are those episodes as morally clear as they initially seem? Or are at least some of them more ambiguous, suggesting that caution is needed in judging conduct that seems at first blush wholly reprehensible? While only preliminary answers to these questions are available, they nonetheless provide a basis for exploring further a neglected but fascinating subject: the idea of the sellout in Black American history.

Let's begin with David Walker's* *Appeal to the Col-*

*David Walker (1785–1830) was born to an enslaved father and a free mother, thus inheriting the status of a free black. He spent much *oured Citizens of the World* (1829). Walker fiercely attacks the cruelty and hypocrisy of the racism of antebellum white America: its subordination of free Negroes up North and its bondage of enslaved Negroes down South. Yet Walker also directs criticisms inward. He repeatedly bewails what he sees as blacks' disgraceful tendency toward communal self-destruction. He denounces free blacks who eschew open opposition to white supremacy in favor of a politics of mere survival. Keenly aware that slaveholders and their allies justified Negro slavery in part on the premise that blacks were "natural" slaves who preferred bondage to freedom, Walker portrayed Negro quiescence as a form of betrayal that reinforced the Negro's degradation. Walker insisted that blacks "have to prove to the Americans and the world that we are MEN, and not *brutes,* as we have been represented, and by millions treated."[1] For free blacks to refrain from engaging in open protest was, in Walker's view, a type of passive betrayal. Had Walker used the lingo popular

---

of his adult life in Boston, where he actively participated in struggles against colonization and slavery. The full title of Walker's pamphlet is *Walker's Appeal, in Four Articles; Together with a Preamble, to the Coloured Citizens of the World, but in Particular, and Very Expressly, to those of the United States of America.* Following its publication, several southern state legislatures enacted laws banning seditious literature and further punishing the education of slaves. In Georgia, a bounty was put on Walker: ten thousand dollars alive, one thousand dollars dead. Walker died in 1830 under mysterious circumstances. Many suspect that he was poisoned. See Peter P. Hinks, *To Awaken My Afflicted Brethren: David Walker and the Problem of Antebellum Slave Resistance* (1997).

today, he would surely have labeled as "sellouts" free blacks who declined to participate actively in struggles on behalf of colored folk.

In his denunciation of African Americans, Walker also targeted those he perceived as perpetrating active betrayal—black participants in the recapture of runaway slaves or blacks who informed white authorities of impending slave revolts. Walker accuses "colored people" of "courting favor with, and telling news and lies to our natural enemies, against each other—aiding them to keep their hellish chains of slavery upon us."[2] He assails blacks "who receive a great portion of their daily bread . . . from the blood and tears of their more miserable brethren, whom they scandalously delivered into the hands of our natural enemies!!!!!"[3] While some of our white friends "are working for our emancipation," Walker exclaims, "we are, by our treachery, wickedness, and deceit, working against ourselves and our children."[4]

Walker's complaint touched upon an important impediment to slave uprisings. There are numerous examples of blacks informing upon or otherwise subverting enslaved rebels. In the Stono Rebellion in South Carolina in 1739, "the most serious slave uprising in colonial America," substantial numbers of slaves assisted their masters in quelling the revolt.[5] A slave named July was commended by a legislative committee for "saving his Master and his Family from being destroyed by the rebellious Negroes." He "bravely fought against the Rebels, and killed one of them." As a reward for his service and an incentive to prompt similar conduct from other slaves, white authorities emancipated July and gave him a suit of clothes, including shoes. Although he was the only slave loyalist to receive his freedom, he was not the only one to attract praise and thanks. Thirty were cited for their loyalty during the rebellion and rewarded with clothing and cash. Some helped to capture and punish the Stono rebels, and a few became rebel-hunters who pursued participants in the uprising.

Subsequently, it became official policy in South Carolina to reward publicly outstanding examples of servile loyalty. It appears that this policy bore fruit. In 1740, when slaves planned an uprising in Berkeley County, a slave named Peter alerted the whites. In 1743, when a group of slaves decided to flee to St. Augustine, Florida, a slave named Sabina revealed their intentions.

In 1800, in Richmond, Virginia, slave informers helped to thwart what might have been one of the largest insurrections in the history of American Negro slavery: Gabriel Prosser's planned rebellion.[6] On the eve of the uprising, several slaves told their masters of the conspiracy. An enslaved informer, moreover, played an instrumental role in Prosser's capture and execution. Prosser sought protection from a white man, a former overseer, who tried to smuggle him to safety aboard a schooner. One of the slaves on the boat, however, recognized Prosser and turned him in to authorities, a service for which he received fifty dollars.[7]*

*A fictional depiction of this thwarted uprising that illuminates the imagined psychology of the enslaved informant is Arna Bontemps's *Black Thunder: Gabriel's Revolt: Virginia, 1800* (1936).

Twelve years later, in New Orleans, a slave named Lewis Bolah learned of an uprising being organized by slaves and free persons of color. Bolah claimed that he was "offered the post of Captain in the operation and assured of being rewarded by freedom and wealth."[8] Instead of assisting the rebellion, however, Bolah helped to destroy it by telling authorities about the impending "horrible conspiracy."*

In June 1822, Denmark Vesey attempted to organize a slave rebellion.[9] He envisioned conquering Charleston, South Carolina, killing the white population, and then escaping by ship to Haiti. Throughout the planning of this undertaking, Vesey was deeply concerned about betrayal. He assured followers that treachery would be repaid with death. He also limited the cadre of lieutenants with whom he worked, largely excluding free

*In February 1813, the Louisiana legislature appropriated $800 for the purchase and subsequent emancipation of Bolah. His enjoyment of freedom, however, was diminished by fear that he would be harmed by vengeful blacks. He could not remain in Louisiana with safety, he complained, "as he had every reason to believe that he might be the victim of disappointed Treason." To get away, he enlisted in the United States Navy. Upon mustering out, he considered moving to Haiti but decided not to out of worry that because of what he had done in New Orleans he would be "an object of persecution in any Society governed by persons of colour." Instead of experiencing liberty as "the greatest boon which could have been bestowed," Bolah, in his isolation, had "only caused him to be an unhappy wanderer." Finally, he returned to his birthplace. But upon reaching Virginia he found that state law forbade free blacks from migrating into the state. Bolah petitioned the Virginia Assembly for an exemption, which it granted. See *A Documentary History of the Negro People in the United States,* ed. Herbert Aptheker (1951, 1990), vol. 1, p. 79.

blacks and mulattoes regardless of their status. Vesey's efforts, however, proved unavailing, as plans of his uprising were revealed to white authorities by a house slave named Peter Prioleau. The South Carolina Assembly enacted special legislation to free Prioleau on Christmas Day of 1822 and to award him a lifetime annual pension of one hundred dollars, which he used to purchase several slaves for himself.[10]

The period that stretched from the abolition of slavery to the consolidation of the Jim Crow regime witnessed many conflicts within Black America that gave rise to claims of racial betrayal. Particularly instructive in this regard are the careers of Martin R. Delany and William Hannibal Thomas.

Delany was born in what is now West Virginia in 1812 to an enslaved black father and a free black mother.[11] He forged several impressive careers. He published the *Mystery,* the first black-run newspaper west of the Alleghenies, and later coedited the *North Star* alongside Frederick Douglass. He was among the first blacks to gain admission to Harvard University when he briefly attended its medical school in 1850 before being forced to leave when school authorities capitulated to the demands of white students who objected to the presence of Negro classmates. He wrote several important texts in which he urged various responses to racial subordination including protest, communal self-help, and immigration. Dubbed the father of black nationalism by enthusiastic readers of his work in the 1960s, Delany wrote, among other things, *The Condition, Elevation, Emigration, and*

Destiny of the Colored People of the United States, Politically Considered (1852) and the novel *Blake, Or the Huts of America* (1859). When the Civil War broke out, Delany urged the Lincoln administration to permit the enlistment of blacks as soldiers and, near the end of the war, himself joined the Union Army as a major, becoming the first African-American field officer.

After the Civil War, Delany moved to South Carolina, where he sought political fortune in the Republican Party. Encountering disappointment, he shifted allegiances. He found himself estranged from the Republican Party, the party of Lincoln and Emancipation, the party that was widely seen as the main political friend of the Negro. He became drawn to the Democratic Party, the political home of many of those who had formerly been slaveholders and secessionists and who, after the Civil War, resisted Reconstruction. Delany's apostasy reached its acme when, in the landmark gubernatorial campaign of 1876, he not only supported but actually campaigned for the Democratic Party candidate Wade Hampton III, a wealthy planter who had been a Confederate general. When Delany traveled to Edisto Island, South Carolina, to address a crowd of blacks on behalf of Hampton, he was drowned out by noise made by people who dismissed him as a "nigger Democrat." The next day, when Delany again campaigned for Democrats, he was denounced by black militiamen in a fashion traditionally reserved for those labeled traitors: he was fired upon, though he escaped injury.

William Hannibal Thomas was born in Ohio in 1843.

Like Delany, Thomas experienced blatant racial discrim ination when he attempted to obtain an education. The first black student to enroll in Otterbein College, he suffered physical and verbal abuse on account of his race and left before earning his degree. An enlistee in the Union Army in the Civil War, Thomas lost an arm in combat but still managed to achieve modest success as a journalist, clergyman, jurist, and politician.

Throughout Reconstruction, Thomas championed efforts to elevate the status of Negroes, continually reminding audiences that "in the hour of their country's danger," Negroes "staked their lives to maintain its honor and integrity, unsullied with treason's stains."[12] He railed against racism, declaring that distinctions based on caste "are incongruous elements that make war continually upon . . . manhood's nobler and spiritual self."[13] In the decade after the fall of Reconstruction, Thomas continued to defend the reputation of the Negro and, in the face of an increasingly violent white supremacist backlash, urged blacks to defend themselves by whatever means necessary. Writing in 1889, he maintained that "the shot-gun, in the hands of a fearless Negro, has no superior as a weapon of defense or as a powerful persuader to right-doing."[14] Alluding to the impunity with which white men raped black women and murdered black men, Thomas averred that "every white contaminator of moral rectitude and lawless iniquity remorselessly shot down at the feet of his Negro victim is a praiseworthy and righteous vindication of Negro manhood."[15]

During the next few years, however, for reasons that are unclear, Thomas's racial beliefs flipped. He came to see blacks as racial inferiors who needed white supervision to overcome their crippling "negro idiosyncrasies." The work in which Thomas most fully set forth this view is *The American Negro: What He Was, What He Is, and What He Will Become: A Critical and Practical Discussion* (1901). Most of the book consists of impressions, unaided by supportive evidence, that put blacks in an almost invariably negative light:

The negro . . . has a mind that never thinks in complex terms; negro intelligence is both superficial and delusive; [the negro] lives wholly in his passions and is never so happy as when enveloped in the glitter and gloss of shams; the negro represents an illiterate race, in which ignorance, cowardice, folly, and idleness are rife, and one whose existence is dominated by emotional sensations; the negro is always an imitator and never a creator; the negro is apparently unable practically to discern between right and wrong; the negro lives only in the present . . . ; The negro represents an intrinsically inferior type of humanity, and one whose predominant characteristics evince an aptitude for a low order of living; negro religious belief . . . enthralls illiterate souls and blindfolds conscience by its methods of false scriptural exegesis; negro religion, by statement and method, strives to stifle in the minds of its followers every intelligent reaching after divine truth; negroes have not learned the elementary principles of moral conduct, nor acquired sobriety of speech, nor delicacy of manner; negro nature is so craven and sensuous in every fibre of its being that a negro manhood with decent respect for chaste womanhood does not exist; innate modesty is not a characteristic of the American negro women; [negro men] have an inordinate craving for carnal knowledge of white women.[16]

To enable blacks to overcome their supposed racial disabilities, Thomas proposed a regimen of white supervision reinforced by physical compulsion. Asserting that there is "common agreement that the evil instincts of negro nature ought to be eradicated," Thomas averred that "when appeals to conscience and reason fail of response, it is our duty to back up such commands for right doing with force."[17] He recommended that blacks be whipped as punishment for minor crimes, and he defended Jim Crow racial distinctions. Maintaining that "the most consummate agent for the redemption of the race will be found in its subjection to a superior white Christian supervision," Thomas insisted that "when negroes are placed under capable white leadership, they become more intelligent in method and more faithful in performance than when left to their own guidance."[18] Demanding "the utter extinction, root and branch, of all negroid beliefs and practices,"[19] he suggested that an optimal way of handling the "negro problem" would be to remove black children from their parents, sever all of their connections with other Negroes, and place them in orphanages in which they could be raised by white guardians.[20]

White supremacists praised *The American Negro.* Thomas Nelson Page lauded it as "perhaps the most remarkable study of the Negro which has appeared. No inconsiderable part of its value is owing to the fact that the author, a free colored man, has had both the power to observe closely and the courage to record boldly the results of his observations."[21] In his polemic *The Negro: A Menace to Civilization,* Robert W. Shufeldt praised Thomas's "excellent" study, which he said displayed "the negro race in its true ethnological light."[22] The *Richmond Dispatch* remarked, "Thirty years is a long time to wait for a prophet of his own race to arise and tell the negro the unvarnished truth but he seems to have come at last, and with a tongue as rough as some Old Testament prophets."[23]

With virtual unanimity, black commentators excoriated the book and sought to ostracize its author. Blacks in Memphis held "an indignation meeting" at which they warned Thomas that he risked physical assault if he ever dared set foot in their city.[24] The writer Charles W. Chesnutt compared Thomas's "traitorous blow" unfavorably to the handiwork of Judas and Benedict Arnold. He then quipped, "[I]f it be any satisfaction to [Thomas] to know that he has not a single friend or well-wisher among the whole eight or ten millions of his own people, he may rest content that such is emphatically the case."[25] Sounding a similar theme, Booker T. Washington concluded his negative review of *The American Negro* by saying, "It is sad to think of a man without a country. It is sadder to think of a man without a race."[26] J. Max Barber, the editor of the *Voice of the Negro,* declared that "Negro children ought to be taught to spit upon [Thomas's] name."[27] In a forty-nine-page pamphlet, Reverend Timothy Tice urged Thomas to "go off and hang thyself," while another critic insisted that "death is too good for him."[28]

Among black leaders of the first rank, none have been more preoccupied with the idea of racial betrayal than Marcus Garvey (1887–1940). Born in Jamaica, Garvey came to the United States in 1916 and founded the Universal Negro Improvement Association and African Communities League (UNIA), which he envisioned as the organizational spine for pan-African unity and, ultimately, a pan-African nation. He "built a steamship line, sponsored colonial expeditions to Liberia [though Garvey himself never reached Africa], staged annual international conventions, inspired businesses, endorsed political candidates, fostered black history and culture, and organized thousands."[29] He "ignited the imagination of a black proletariat disappointed by the promises of urban immigration and frustrated by racial injustice."[30] A subject of contention in his own lifetime, Garvey remains controversial today. But the considerable esteem with which he is remembered by many black Americans is mirrored by the first line of a profile on Garvey authored by Professors Henry Louis Gates, Jr., and Cornel West: "Marcus Garvey was the Moses of twentieth-century black folk."[31]

A feature of Garvey's thinking that is often minimized is the stress he placed on what he perceived as black racial treachery. Observing that oppressed peoples have always been encumbered by traitors, Garvey asserted that blacks "are more encumbered in this way than any other race in the world."[32] While the traitors of other races are generally confined to the mediocre or the irresponsible, Garvey maintained, "the traitors among the Negro race are generally to be found among the men highest placed in education and society, the fellows who call themselves leaders."[33]*

Garvey often broadly denounced whole occupations in making his charges of racial subversion. The purpose of most Negro intellectuals, he scoffed, "is to deceive the less fortunate of his race, and, by his wiles ride easily into position and wealth at their expense."[34] "Negro race leaders," he insisted, "are the biggest crooks in the world. . . . You can pay the Negro leader to hang his race and block every effort of self-help."[35] The Negro press, he charged, "is the most venal, ignorant and corrupt of our time. . . . You may purchase its policy and destroy or kill any professed ideal if you would make the offer in cash."[36] Garvey similarly chastised black entrepreneurs, alleging that blacks were developing a class of "money-hoarders" that was "much more dangerous to the race's life and existence than any similar group of men among any other race. . . . The [black] rich are selfish and fool-

---

*"[W]e have more traitors than leaders," Garvey complained, "because nearly everyone who essays to lead the race . . . does so by first establishing himself as the pet of some philanthropist of another race, to whom he will go and debase his race in the worst form, humiliate his own manhood, and thereby win the sympathy of the 'great benefactor' who will dictate to him what he should do in the leadership of the Negro race." *Philosophy and Opinions of Marcus Garvey*, edited by Amy Jacques-Garvey, with an introduction by Robert A. Hill (1923, 1992), vol. 1, p. 29.

ish, and their primary purpose in life is to ape the whites, and as quickly as possible seek their company with the hope of social absorption, and jumping over the race line. Any ordinary rich Negro or 'colored' person would prefer to give away ninety-nine and one-half percent of his wealth to become white, rather than to remain as he is, and to use such wealth in the promotion of racial ideals or industry that would help the mass of his people."[37]

Garvey similarly assailed Negro organizations, particularly the National Association for the Advancement of Colored People. Asserting that its leaders "have as much love for the Negro blood in their veins as the devil has for holy water," Garvey charged that the NAACP "is a scheme to destroy the Negro Race."[38]*

The individual that Garvey condemned most bitterly was W. E. B. DuBois. In Garvey's view, DuBois exemplified the effete, untrustworthy, mulatto elite that claimed to be committed to the elevation of the Negro community but actually yearned to escape from it to a sheltered existence within white America. Garvey purported to dismiss DuBois from the Negro race on the ground that he was "an enemy of the black people of the world"[39]†—

---

*As between the Ku Klux Klan and the NAACP, Garvey asserted that he preferred the former "for their honesty of purpose toward the Negro. They are better friends to my race, for telling us what they are, and what they mean, thereby giving us a chance to stir for ourselves, than all the hypocrites put together with their false gods and religions, notwithstanding." *Philosophy and Opinions of Marcus Garvey,* vol. 2, p. 71.

†Garvey was fond of seeking to dismiss from the black fold various Negro ideological opponents. He charged that Cyril V. Briggs, the

a charge that DuBois threw right back at Garvey when he
declared that his antagonist was "either a lunatic or a
traitor" and that, in any event, Garvey was "without
doubt, the most dangerous enemy of the Negro race in
America and the world."[40]

DuBois was not alone in this appraisal of Garvey, and
some who agreed with him engaged in conduct that
would, if engaged in currently, undoubtedly be labeled
as "selling out." In the 1920s, the United States Bureau
of Investigation, the precursor to the Federal Bureau of
Investigation, used black agents to infiltrate Garvey's
Universal Negro Improvement Association. One, James
Wormley Jones, became an officer in the organization
who supplied the Bureau with all sorts of information,
including a list of subscribers to the *Negro World*, Garvey's principal newspaper. Black agents so adeptly penetrated the UNIA that at one point Garvey found himself
unknowingly appealing to one undercover operative for
help in dealing with another![41]*

---

leader of the African Blood Brotherhood for African Liberation and
Redemption, was not a black man but was only a "Negro for con-
venience." Briggs sued for libel and won a judgment that was paid
for by the sale of one of Garvey's ships. See David Levering Lewis,
*W. E. B. DuBois: The Fight for Equality and the American Century,
1919–1963*, (2000), p. 74.
*Garvey himself was not above attempting to use the United States
government to destroy rivals. In 1923, he wired the United States
attorney general to contrast what he portrayed as the patriotism of
the UNIA with the subversiveness of competitors. He labeled as
"a red Socialistic organization" a group entitled The Friends of
Negro Freedom and accused the African Blood Brotherhood of being

We have seen that Garvey denounced DuBois as a race traitor. He was not the only one to do so. The distinguished activist Archibald Grimké (1849–1930) was among others who, on at least one occasion, challenged DuBois's faithfulness to the black community. During World War I, DuBois published a column, "Close Ranks," in which he urged blacks to subordinate to the war effort their many justified complaints. "Let us," DuBois asserted, "forget our special grievances and close our ranks shoulder to shoulder with our own fellow white citizens and the allied nations that are fighting for democracy."[42] Grimké opposed this stance, which he viewed as all too acquiescent, given the United States's mistreatment of blacks, including Negro soldiers, and its flagrant indifference to lynching and other lawless outrages openly perpetrated against African Americans by state governments and private parties. In contrast to DuBois's unequivocal expression of wartime support, Grimké wondered aloud whether it made sense for blacks "to send their sons and brothers to make the world safe for democracy when America, their home, is not safe for them."[43] "The German," Grimké noted, "can travel in a Pullman, he can eat in a first-class hotel . . . he can enjoy all other luxuries for which he is able and willing to pay, while we [blacks] who shed our blood for democracy are treated worse than dogs."[44]

"representatives of the Bolsheviki of Russia." Quoted in E. David Cronon, *Black Moses: The Story of Marcus Garvey and the Universal Negro Improvement Association* (1968), p. 198.

While Grimké's anger at DuBois stemmed from ideological disagreement, it also arose from a belief that DuBois had been corrupted by the desire to obtain an appointment as a military officer. Objecting to DuBois's attempt to serve simultaneously as a captain in military intelligence and as the editor of the NAACP's journal, the *Crisis,* Grimké led a faction that denounced DuBois as a Benedict Arnold.[45]* Similarly dismissive was William Monroe Trotter (1872–1934), a militant African-American crusader for racial equality who often sided with DuBois in struggles with Booker T. Washington and other accomodationists. On this occasion, however, Trotter called DuBois "a rank quitter of the fight for our rights." At the very time, he complained, "when the greatest opportunity is at hand" during "the war for democracy for all others," DuBois "has at last finally weakened, compromised, deserted the fight, betrayed the cause of his race."[46]

Were the damning assessments of Grimké and Trotter accurate? Some students of DuBois think so. According to David Levering Lewis, DuBois's most comprehensive biographer, "'Close Ranks' was unworthy [of him] not

---

*Fear also accounts in part for DuBois's conduct. Explaining why he declined to publish in the *Crisis* a poem in which Grimke dramatized and condemned racist mistreatment of black soldiers, DuBois candidly noted: "We have just been *specially warned* by the Department of Justice that some of our articles are considered disloyal. I would not dare, therefore, to print this [poem] just now." Dickson D. Bruce, *Archibald Grimké: Portrait of a Black Independent* (1993), p. 224.

because [it] could not have been honorably defended on its own terms, but because what he wrote was in large part written in order to consummate [a] bargain [with the government]."[47]*

During the civil-rights revolution of the 1950s and 1960s, leading black figures constantly addressed themselves to what they saw as the problem of racial betrayal by complacency, collaboration, or outright treachery. Fannie Lou Hamer declared that the champions of black empowerment had to "stop the . . . Toms" from selling out. "I don't believe in killing," she remarked, "but a good whipping behind the bushes wouldn't hurt them."[48] Malcolm X asserted that "just as the slavemaster [in the days of slavery] used Tom, the house Negro, to keep the field Negroes in check, the same old slavemaster today has Negroes who are nothing but modern Uncle Toms—twentieth century Uncle Toms—to keep you and me in check."[49] "There are Negroes," Martin Luther King, Jr., complained, "who will never fight for freedom. There are Negroes who will seek profit for themselves

---

*Professor Lewis's interpretation is controversial. For a defense of DuBois that rejects the suggestion that he was improperly influenced by the prospect of receiving an appointment, see William Jordan, "The Damnable Dilemma: African-American Accommodation and Protest During World War I," 81 *Journal of American History* 1562 (1995). For an interpretation supportive of Lewis's view, see Mark Ellis, "'Closing Ranks' and 'Seeking Honors': W. E. B. DuBois in World War I," 79 *Journal of American History* 96 (1992), and "W. E. B. DuBois and the Formation of Black Opinion in World War I: A Commentary on 'The Damnable Dilemma,'" 81 *Journal of American History* 1584 (1995).

alone from the struggle. There are even some Negroes who will cooperate with their oppressors."[50]

King and the others were speaking about an aspect of the civil-rights revolution that is underappreciated: the extent to which those who challenged the white supremacist racial status quo had to contend with not only white but also black enemies. In Mississippi, for example, segregationists created an organization, the Mississippi State Sovereignty Commission, whose primary purpose was to "protect" the state against challenges to white supremacy. To advance that aim, the Commission recruited blacks to serve as its "eyes and ears." Reverend H. H. Humes, a Baptist minister, attended civil-rights meetings in Greenville, Mississippi, and dutifully reported on them to his handlers at the Sovereignty Commission. When the Regional Council of Negro Leadership met in April 1957, Humes paid a Negro stenographer to make a verbatim transcript of the proceedings, which he then forwarded to the Commission. Happy to receive this information, particularly insofar as it recorded an apparent failure, a leading figure at the Commission wrote, alluding to Humes and other "good" Negroes, that "we owe a debt [of] gratitude to our negro friends who have been cooperating so fully." It was largely due to their work, he continued, "that this wildly ballyhoo[ed] meeting of agitators was such a grand flop."[51] When the great hero of the Mississippi civil-rights movement, Medgar Evers, addressed meetings in Greenville or nearby towns, Reverend Humes would be on hand to keep tabs on what was said and done.

Civil-rights activists denounced Humes when journalists exposed his connection with the Commission as a paid informant. The Ministerial Improvement Association of Mississippi adopted a resolution asserting that he was "unworthy of the fellowship of the ministers of the Protestant denominations in Mississippi" and could no longer "speak for Mississippi Negroes."[52] And the NAACP's executive director, Roy Wilkins, denounced him as a traitor who was "quick to get [his] hands in the till."[53]

Fear of ostracism, however, did not deter other blacks from emulating Humes. Fred H. Miller of Mound Bayou, Mississippi, compiled for the Commission a list of Negroes whom he believed to be members of the NAACP. B. L. Bell, the principal of a black elementary school in Cleveland, Mississippi, sought a position with the Commission and received favorable attention after his boss, the Bolivar County Superintendent of Schools, lauded him as a "white man's Negro."[54] Bell, too, routinely informed Commission officials of the identities, addresses, telephone numbers, and birthdays of people suspected of being members of the NAACP. Indeed, Bell harbored ambitions to become more than a paid informant. He envisioned creating a secret society of like-minded blacks who would oppose civil-rights activists in order to preserve "the present way of life in Mississippi."[55] At an initial meeting, Bell and his confederates agreed that they would help the Commission by "handling any incident or developments that might threaten segregation."[56] But the organization failed to jell, and by

1960, Bell's career as a black covert agent for segregation was over.

Although the problem of defection has received notably little attention in the voluminous literature on the civil-rights movement, the reality is that spying and other forms of subversion constantly menaced the insurgents. In Birmingham, Alabama, Charles "Rat Killer" Barnett, a black petty criminal, conveyed information as a paid informant to the infamous police chief Bull Connor.[57] From 1963 to 1968, Jim Harrison, a black accountant hired by the Southern Christian Leadership Conference (SCLC), regularly supplied federal authorities with information about that organization and its charismatic leader.[58] Black undercover agents of the Memphis Police Department infiltrated the Black Organizing Project (BOP), which constituted part of the coalition of groups that sought to support sanitation workers during their strike in Memphis, Tennessee, in 1968—the mass mobilization punctuated by the assasination of Martin Luther King, Jr.[59]

This use of black spies to maintain surveillance of black activists was ongoing, systematic, and extensive. In 1967, the FBI launched a "Ghetto Informant Program" aimed at enabling officials to monitor the tenor of public opinion in black communities. By the summer of 1968, the FBI had hired some 3,248 individuals to develop its "ghetto listening posts."[60] Under the direction of the FBI, black spies and agents provocateurs penetrated virtually all of the significant black activist organizations. A common ploy used to disrupt these organizations involved spreading rumors that this or that activist had "sold out." This ploy worked spectacularly well against the Black Panther Party (BPP).

> Everybody distrusted everyone else in Panther chapters. Everyone believed that the offices were crawling with spies. Pantherdom had become a hall of mirrors: anyone might be a spy, and few seemed totally trustworthy. The FBI ... relied on two kinds of helpers. The first kind were their own spies, passing as real Panthers. The second kind were loyal Panthers whom the FBI had "bad-jacketed" by inserting false rumors of *dis*loyalty.[61]

The consequences for the Panthers were catastrophic. They became consumed with weeding out traitors, falling prey to a collective paranoia that led to constant purgings and at least one murder of a member charged with disloyalty: in 1969, a group of Black Panthers in New Haven, Connecticut, killed a comrade, Alex Rackley, wrongly believing him to be an informant.

Similarly tragic is the story of William O'Neal.[62] While incarcerated in the Cook County Jail, O'Neal was instructed by an agent in the FBI's Racial Matters squad to infiltrate the Chicago Panthers. He did so and was soon put in charge of the Panthers' security. Thereafter he did all sorts of things to undermine the organization. He falsely accused a member of a gang, the Vice Lords, of being a police informant in order to scuttle a proposed alliance with the Panthers. He encouraged the distribution of racist, antiwhite cartoons to create a rift between the Panthers and the Students for a Democratic

Society (SDS). He encouraged Panthers to pursue criminal activities in order to discredit the organization and to create an excuse for police action facilitated by O'Neal's spying—work for which the FBI paid him one hundred dollars to five hundred dollars monthly.

In November 1969, O'Neal told law-enforcement authorities that illegal weapons were being stored in an apartment frequented by Fred Hampton, the charismatic twenty-one-year-old leader of the Chicago Panthers. Soon thereafter, when local and federal anthorities raided the apartment, shooting erupted. Hampton was among those killed.

O'Neal received a three-hundred-dollar bonus from the FBI for his assistance. He appears, however, to have paid a high price for his role. To avoid retaliation, O'Neal had to enter the federal Witness Protection Program. Then, in January 1990, he committed suicide. While a full explanation for O'Neal's self-destruction is unavailable, it seems that remorse over his role as an FBI informant probably played some part in the despondency that prompted him to take his own life.

Much of the conduct that gave rise to the episodes recounted above was unequivocally wrong, a product of jealousy, greediness, hatred, bigotry, and all manner of other baleful failings. As this neglected feature of African-American history is more fully explored, however, it should be kept in mind that even conduct that might seem at first blush to constitute a simple case of "selling out" may, upon further scrutiny, turn out to be ambiguous. Consider a slave who informs his master of the plans of another slave to mount a rebellion. On the face of it, this looks like the paradigmatic sellout. But just suppose the informant has previously sought to persuade the rebel that his plans for an uprising are woefully deficient. Just suppose that the informer presciently recognizes that if the rebel proceeds with his attempt at an uprising it will not only fail but will precipitate a sharp increase in the suffering imposed on the slave community, including the dismemberment of enslaved families by an enraged owner who had previously been, in relative terms, a rather lenient master. Let's also suppose that the dominant motive animating the informer is protecting the slave community (which includes a spouse and children) and not a strictly selfish aim. Under these circumstances, what might at first seem to be an act of simple betrayal is actually something much more complex—a betrayal stemming from loyalty to an entire enslaved community. One might disagree with the choice made by the hypothesized informant. It seems wrong, however, to view him or her contemptuously as merely selling out.*

---

*We know little about the motivations of enslaved informants. Enough is known about American slavery and analogous circumstances to believe, however, that situations of the sort I hypothesize actually occurred. In a letter to the governor of South Carolina in 1793, an anonymous black sounded alarms about an impending rebellion. He said that he was prompted to act in the hope of "saving the blood of his fellow creatures." Who he considered his "fellow creatures" is unclear, but may have included other black folk. See *A Documentary History of the Negro People in the United States,* Herbert Aptheker, ed. (1951, 1990), p. 29.

Or consider the case of the informants who spied on Marcus Garvey's UNIA. At least with respect to some of them, motives other than self-serving advancement appear to have been at work. Some spoke of ideological antipathy to the UNIA and fears that the dictatorial Garvey would impetuously inflame race relations to the detriment of black Americans. Such sentiments were shared by a number of prominent, widely respected blacks who openly cheered or assisted with Garvey's prosecution, conviction, and deportation. Among this array were Robert S. Abbott, the editor of the legendary *Chicago Defender*; Cyril Briggs, the founder of the African Blood Brotherhood for African Liberation and Redemption; and leading figures in the National Association for the Advancement of Colored People. If a person relayed information on Garvey to government officials because the self-described Black Moses had become, in DuBois's words, "the most dangerous enemy of the Negro race in America and the world," it is hard to see why such conduct should be denounced as wrongful treachery. Indeed, if, after investigation, one were to concur with DuBois's assessment, the conduct of an anti-Garvey informant might well be said to warrant applause rather than condemnation.*

---

*In his careful exposition of the federal government's surveillance of black organizations in the 1920s, Professor Theodore Kornweibel expressly refrains from condemning the black informants. "[T]he African American population was then, as it is now, large and diverse, with a multiplicity of political viewpoints. Marcus Garvey is today widely honored, but in the 1920s his sizeable following was

The same analysis might well require revision of long-established assessments of certain purported villains of the civil-rights revolution. As things stand, many people would disparagingly label as a sellout any black person who, during the '60s or '70s, assisted or even merely cooperated with law-enforcement authorities engaged in investigating black protesters. Alongside the noble figures and exemplary deeds of the Second Reconstruction, however, were base criminals and appalling misconduct that warranted governmental intervention.[63] The Black Panther Party in particular presents the problem of an organization that was in part admirably heroic and in part despicably thuggish. Given the presence of rogue elements within the BPP, criminals whose misconduct not only discredited that organization but also posed a menace to the goals of the black-liberation struggle as a whole, is it not clear that, in at least some circumstances, assisting law enforcement constituted a benefit, not a detriment, to the cause of black communal betterment? A comprehensive response will have to await additional research and reflection. For now it is enough that the matter be put forward as a legitimate, serious question.

---

counterbalanced by many who sincerely believed he was dangerously misleading the race." Theodore Kornweibel, Jr., *"Seeing Red": Federal Campaigns Against Black Militancy, 1919–1925* (1998), p. xiii.

Three

The Idea of the Sellout in Contemporary Black America

*"[T]raitors are much worse than adversaries; for
every nation hates most the betrayer from within."*

Stephen L. Carter, *Reflections of an
Affirmative Action Baby* (1991)

Angst over complacency, collaboration, and defection
continues to occupy a salient place in the Afro-American
mind and soul. One hears it in ceaselessly repeated
phrases such as "Don't forget where you come from"
and "Stay black." One sees it in the often obsessive attentiveness with which many blacks scrutinize other blacks
for evidence of "passing," "acting white,"* or otherwise
showing what is denounced as an inadequate commit-

---

* "Acting white" is a derogatory term meant to stigmatize blacks who
are said to betray the expectations of their own racial group by assim-
ilating the expectations of white society. This use of the term has itself
been harshly criticized, since it disparages as "white" such socially
useful traits as studiousness, academic ambitiousness, attentiveness to
proper grammar, and respect for other conventional protocols. That
there exists among certain groups of blacks peer pressure to avoid
"acting white" is clear. Controversial, however, is the extent of the
stigmatization for "acting white." The contentious literature on the

ment to black solidarity. One sees it in efforts by blacks, especially those in elite, predominantly white settings, to signal to other blacks (and themselves as well) that they have remained true to blackness. These efforts, according to journalist John Blake, have given rise to "the Soul Patrol . . . thought police who enforce conformity." Soul Patrols, he contends, are constituted by "the legions of black people who impose their definition of blackness on other black people." Obnoxiously intrusive, they aren't content with choosing your friends, he complains. "They want to tell you how to think, where to live, whom to love, how to do your job."[1]

Concern over selling out surfaces in the lyrics of "No Sell Out" by the gangsta rap group the Geto Boys. It pervades writings that ask whether affluent blacks have an obligation to reside in black communities, whether blacks have an obligation to marry within the race, whether black professionals have an obligation to embrace certain opportunities while avoiding others, whether black intellectuals have special, racial, responsibilities and,

---

"acting white" phenomenon is large. For starters, see Prudence L. Carter, *Keepin' It Real: School Success Beyond Black and White* (2005); John Ogbu and Astrid Davis, *Black American Students in an Affluent Suburb: A Study of Academic Disengagement* (2003); Roland G. Fryer, Jr. (with Paul Torelli), "An Empirical Analysis of 'Acting White,'" Harvard University and the National Bureau of Economic Research (NBER), Oct. 7, 2006; Philip Cook and Jens Ludwig, "The Burden of 'Acting White': Do Black Adolescents Disparage Academic Achievement?," in *The Black-White Test Score Gap*, Christopher Jencks and Meredith Phillips, eds. (1998).

if they do, whether they are discharging their duties properly.*

Concern over selling out assumes center stage in the movie *Drop Squad* (1994), which chronicles a gang that kidnaps perceived "sellouts" and tries to compel them to become "good"—that is to say, dutiful—"brothers" and "sisters." It is also at the core of Spike Lee's film *Bamboozled* (2000), which dramatizes the murder of a black entertainer executed for demeaning African Americans. African-American novelists have repeatedly grappled with the idea of the sellout. Sutton Griggs did so at the dawn of the twentieth century in *Imperium in Imperio*

*See, e.g., Eugene Rivers, "On the Responsibility of Intellectuals in the Age of Crack," *Boston Review,* Sept./Oct. 1992; bell hooks, Eugene Rivers, Randall Kennedy, Regina Austin, Selwyn Cudjoe, Glenn Loury, "Do Black Intellectuals Have Special Obligations?," *Boston Review,* Feb./March 1994; Bill E. Lawson, "Uplifting the Race: Middle-Class Blacks and the Truly Disadvantaged," in *The Underclass Question,* Bill E. Lawson, ed. (1992); Alvin F. Poussaint, "The Price of Success: Remembering Their Roots Burdens Many Blacks in Mainstream with Feelings of Either Guilt or Denial," *Ebony,* Aug. 1987; Bebe Moore Campbell, "Staying in the Community," *Essence,* Dec. 1989: Isabel Wilkerson, "Middle-Class Blacks Try to Grip the Ladder While Lending a Hand," *New York Times,* Nov. 26, 1990; Charles W. Mills, "Do Black Men Have a Moral Duty to Marry Black Women?," 25 *Journal of Social Philosophy* 131 (1994); Anita Allen, "Interracial Marriage: Folk Ethics in Contemporary Philosophy," in *Women of Color and Philosophy,* Naomi Zack, ed. (2000); Audrey Edwards, "Bring Me Home a Black Girl," *Essence,* Nov. 2002; David B. Wilkins, "Social Engineers or Corporate Tools? *Brown v. Board of Education* and the Conscience of the Black Corporate Bar," in *Race, Law and Culture: Reflections on Brown v. Board of Education,* Austin Sarat, ed. (1997).

(1899). His story of a thwarted conspiracy to capture Texas and Louisiana begins with a confession. "I am a traitor," the informer declares. "I have betrayed the immediate plans of the race to which I belong." Ralph Ellison explored the problem of racial betrayal at mid-century in the most celebrated novel in the African-American literary canon. In *Invisible Man* (1952), Ellison conjures the specter of the sellout through his depiction of the villainous Dr. Bledsoe, who is willing to do virtually anything to reinforce his dictatorial power at the all-black college over which he presides. I didn't make the American racial problem, Bledsoe declares, "and I know that I can't change it. But I've made my place in it and I'll have every Negro in the country hanging on tree limbs by morning if it means staying where I am." At the end of the century, Sterling Anthony confronts the sellout phenomenon at the opposite extreme by showing the sometimes pathological reactions triggered by perceived betrayals. In *Cookie Cutter* (1999), Anthony creates a black serial killer who murders Negroes he pegs as race traitors.*

A wide range of conduct prompts charges of selling out. In some circumstances, the offense is inaction. It is on this basis that the pan-Africanist advocate Randall Robinson castigated Vernon Jordan, the civil-rights activist turned super-lawyer who became President William Jefferson Clinton's widely publicized friend, golfing

---

*Other novels in which the theme of racial betrayal is prominent include *Black Thunder* (1936) by Arna Bontemps and *Stranger and Alone* (1950) by J. Saunders Redding.

partner, and confidant. Disappointed by what he saw as
Jordan's risk-averse unwillingness to pressure Clinton
regarding United States policy toward Haiti, Robinson
determined that Jordan had fallen prey to a peculiar pathology that causes blacks to slight their communal obligations. Robinson dubbed this pathology "Vernon Jordan
disease, a degenerative condition among blacks . . . that
results in a loss of memory of what they came [to a given
position or institution to accomplish]."[2]

If certain forms of inaction are seen as failures to pay
racial dues, so, too, are certain forms of action. One that
is certain to elicit charges of selling out is marrying a
white person. Consider the assertion of Professor Hal-
ford Fairchild: "For black men to date and marry white
women in the face of our lingering debt to each other is
irresponsible. The brother [who dates or marries interra-
cially] has sold out. We have a responsibility to each
other. We are under siege. We are at war. To sleep with
the enemy is treason. Racial treason."[3]

While Fairchild expressed himself in an extreme fashion, the sentiments he voiced are by no means idiosyn-
cratic. His claim that marrying a white person constitutes
an act of racial betrayal is common among African
Americans. Noting how he and his friends regularly
engage in "race checking," Lawrence Otis Graham
observes:

> We flip through glowing profiles [about successful blacks]
> in *People, Ebony,* or *Business Week* quietly praising the lat-
> est black trailblazer and role model. Then we look for what
> we consider the final determinant of this person's black

identity—the thing that will allow us to bestow our unqualified appreciation. We look for the litmus test of loyalty to the race: the photo of the person's spouse or significant other.[4]

When a black person "fails" this test, Graham and his friends (and many like-minded African Americans) demote the person in question. This sentiment has deep historical roots. Even as esteemed a figure as Frederick Douglass encountered bitter resentment in 1884 when he married a white woman, Helen Pitts. Douglass had previously been married to a black woman, Anna Murray Douglass, for nearly forty-four years. Their relationship produced five children and ended only when Anna died. Still, when Douglass remarried across the race line (two years after Anna's death), many blacks denounced him. A column published in a black-owned newspaper vividly reflects the widely felt sense of hurt: "Fred Douglass has married a red-head white girl. . . . We have no further use for him. His picture [has hung] in our parlor, we will [now] hang it in the stable."[5]*

The "sleeping white" critique remains widespread and potent. The writer Jake Lamar notes that his mother "kept a shit list of black celebrities who had white wives or girlfriends."[6] At or near the top of such lists today is

---

*"Marrying white" is not always portrayed in a negative light. Sex or marriage across racial lines has also been championed as an assertion of racial egalitarianism. See Randall Kennedy, *Interracial Intimacies: Sex, Marriage, Identity, and Adoption* (2003).

Justice Clarence Thomas, one of many prominent black men married to white women.* When Thomas was nominated to succeed Thurgood Marshall on the Supreme Court, some blacks paid much attention to his interracial marriage. Professor Russell Adams of the Howard University Department of Afro-American Studies was quoted as remarking, for example, that Thomas's "marrying of a white woman is a sign of his rejection of the black community."[7]

Pursuing certain occupations or attending to certain tasks within an occupation have prompted charges of selling out. Blacks who serve as police officers can expect such denunciation,† as can blacks who work as elite cor-

---

*There exist many such lists. See, for example, *The American Directory of Certified Uncle Toms*, 222–24 (2002). Blacks who have had nonblack "significant others" include such figures as Kareem Abdul-Jabbar, James Baldwin, Harry Belafonte, Julian Bond, James Brown, Marian Wright Edelman, Ella Fitzgerald, Lorraine Hansberry, Charlie Parker, Gordon A. Parks, Sidney Poitier, Richard Pryor, Franklin Raines, August Wilson, and Richard Wright. One must be careful, however, in relying upon such lists. I found myself listed because of my marriage to Yvedt L. Matory. She was apparently thought to be white or, at least, other than black. See Robert Fikes, Jr., "An Extensive List of Notable Black/Non-Black Interracial Couples, 1801–2001," afrocentricnews.com. My wonderful, beautiful, fabulous wife, who died tragically in 2005, was indeed a black American.

†See Nina Shapiro, "Black and Blue," *Seattle Weekly*, June 20, 2001; Tatsha Robertson, "Caught in the Middle; Black Officers Say They Aren't Accepted at Work or in Community," *Star Tribune* (Minneapolis), Aug. 1, 1993. See also Bobb Hamilton, "Poem to a Nigger Cop," in Leroi Jones and Larry Neal, *Black Fire: An Anthology of Afro-American Writing* (1968), p. 452.

porate attorneys.* During the murder trial of O. J. Simpson, the black assistant district attorney Christopher Darden became a target for accusations of racial betrayal.[8] Black journalists, too, have been condemned. When Milton Coleman of the *Washington Post* revealed that presidential contender Jesse Jackson had referred to Jews as "Hymies," Coleman "was assailed by blacks across the country as a sellout who, for career advancement, was attempting to derail Jackson's historic campaign."[9] Minister Louis Farrakhan of the Nation of Islam vilified the reporter as "a no-good, filthy traitor" who should be shunned "so that he cannot enter in among black people."[10]

Scores of black conservatives have been derided as sellouts. Infuriated by the positions taken by the lone black Republican then sitting in the Congress, a commentator in *Black Enterprise* accused Representative Gary Franks of harboring "racially traitorous views."[11]† Angered by the black economist Thomas Sowell's opposition to affirmative action and other liberal policies, the

---

*Anxieties over selling out in elite law practices have been the emotional and psychological backdrop to an illuminating series of articles by my colleague David Wilkins. See "Identities and Roles: Race, Recognition, and Professional Responsibility," 57 *Maryland Law Review* 1502 (1998); "Social Engineers or Corporate Tools? *Brown v. Board of Education,* and the Conscience of the Black Corporate Bar," in Austin Sarat, ed., *Race, Law and Culture: Reflections on* Brown v. Board of Education (1997).

†Some members of the Congressional Black Caucus urged the expulsion of Representative Franks from the group. For example, Congressman William Clay asserted that Franks should be expelled

journalist Carl Rowan said of him that "Vidkun Quisling, in his collaboration with the Nazis, surely did not
do as much damage to the Norwegians as Sowell is doing
to the most helpless of black Americans. Sowell is giving
aid and comfort to America's racists."[12]* Enraged by
Glenn Loury's opposition to affirmative action (Loury
has subsequently changed his mind), Reverend Benjamin
Hooks, then the executive director of the NAACP,
described the professor's views as "treasonous."[13] In-
censed by what he perceived as an unfeeling conde-
scension toward poor black folk, William Jelani Cobb
described the linguist John McWhorter as "the very definition of a sellout."[14] Outraged by what they perceived
as a disgusting combination of power-grubbing obse-
quiousness, the editors of the Black Commentator
charged that Secretary of State Condoleezza Rice "is the
purest expression of the race traitor."[15] Angered by what
he saw as Reverend Jesse Lee Peterson's "merciless
delight in denigrating other black people," Professor
Michael Eric Dyson labeled the pastor a "racial parasite . . . in the service of white supremacy."[16]

Blacks on the right have also accused black progres-
sives of selling out, claiming that black liberal activists

---

because his political commitments were "inimical to the permanent
interests of black folk." See Kenneth J. Cooper, "Black Caucus's Odd
Man In," *Washington Post*, Sept. 1, 1993.

*The phrase "aid and comfort" is part of the definition of treason set
forth in the United States Constitution, Article III, Section 3: "Treason
against the United States shall consist only in levying War against
them, or in adhering to their Enemies, giving them Aid and Comfort."

and intellectuals have forsaken independence in return for monetary and other benefits supplied by the Democratic Party, universities, and the civil-rights establishment. Tired of being assailed as race traitors, black conservatives are increasingly turning the tables, charging that "the real sellouts" in black communities are criminals, irresponsible fathers of neglected children, purveyors of cultural products that demoralize and demonize black youth, and those who refuse to confront self-destructive tendencies in Black America.[17]*

Although conservatives have succeeded occasionally in effectively deploying sellout rhetoric, for the most part it remains a terminology more of the left than the right. Conservatives' use of that rhetoric, however, serves to spread and deepen its overall influence.

Anxiety over free riding, abandonment, and defection is so widespread within African-American communities that, with certain exceptions, the black who succeeds in a multiracial setting must constantly contend with suspicions harbored by other blacks that his or her success derives, at least in part, from "selling out." This suspi-

---

*This redefinition of racial betrayal is also propounded by African Americans who are not speaking from the Right. See, for example, Jeremy Levitt, "Biggest Sellouts Are Blacks Who Destroy Their Communities," *Chicago Sun-Times,* June 2, 2007 ("[W]e need a new paradigm of selling out. Today's sellouts are blacks who perpetrate violence and destruction in the black community and participate in the globalization of negative stereotypes and images of African Americans"); Bryan Burwell, "Vick Is Latest to Take the Rap for Rap in Our Culture," *St. Louis Post-Dispatch,* July 20, 2007 (black criminals are "the real sellouts").

cion often rubs up against another tendency prevalent in Black America: the habit of celebrating any promotion by a fellow black as a sign of collective advancement. Indeed, in many settings the celebratory impulse is stronger than its rival. When Clarence Thomas was nominated for a seat on the Supreme Court the two tendencies were put directly at odds. Some blacks championed him almost solely because he was "a brother," while others suspected or opposed him because of his conservative sponsorship. On that occasion, the former tendency prevailed. Still, the charge of betrayal is a ubiquitous presence even amid the applause for successful blacks. Rare, indeed, is the successful African American who has not had to evade, preempt, or confront such charges.

What are the effects of the use of sellout rhetoric and the sentiments that attend it? The consequences that have garnered the most attention are negative. Professor Stephen L. Carter complains that the deeply personal vituperation that often erupts in intraracial disputes among black Americans discourages candid expression of views. He maintains that, at least with respect to certain topics, most notably affirmative action, a prevailing orthodoxy exerts undue pressure, stigmatizing dissident positions to such an extent that people holding heterodox ideas either silence themselves or speak out knowing that they will pay a frightful price with their reputations. "I worry," he writes, "about the message conveyed by the righteous fury that many of the current leaders of the black community direct towards dissenters from the traditional civil rights agenda."[18] That message, in Carter's view, is that an African American becomes a race traitor if he or she dissents from liberal civil-rights orthodoxy. Such dissenters, he claims, face the prospect of being "purged." Maintaining that "few Western-style purges are more disheartening, and more threatening to freedom, than the disdainful treatment of intellectuals who dare to challenge fashionable academic orthodoxy," he posits that "a particularly tragic example of this treatment is the isolation of intellectual dissenters who happen to be black."[19]

While Carter focuses on the injuries ostracism inflicts upon the individual who is labeled a sellout, Glenn Loury focuses on the injuries that ostracism of dissidents inflicts upon blacks as a group. Whereas Carter is mainly concerned with the loss of freedom suffered by individual black dissidents, Loury is mainly concerned with the collective burden borne by black communities when potentially productive dialogue is constrained by undue peer pressure. The central injury, as Loury sees it, is the truncation of debate about controversial and complex issues facing black communities. Sensible responses to these issues require careful, disciplined, and robust debate. But according to Loury such debate is all too often foreclosed by "a false, enervating conception of racial loyalty" that is enforced by "self-appointed guardians of racial virtue" who deploy group ostracism to impose an African-American political correctness. Decrying an "intellectual malaise" characterized by excessive self-censorship,

Loury claims that black American thinkers and activists "have fallen prey to what amounts to a conspiracy of silence" about a variety of topics, including "the social and moral condition of the black lower classes." Behind the silence is fear—fear of running afoul of racial party lines. Black elites, Loury charges, "are fearful of engaging in a candid appraisal [of the African-American condition] because they do not want to appear to be disloyal to the race." This "has serious negative consequences for the ability of blacks [to grapple with the real problems that they face]."[20] Far from assisting black communities, the deployment of sellout rhetoric has created a "loyalty trap" that discourages debate and thus facilitates the loss of valuable information and insight. In Loury's view, sellout rhetoric and its attendant sentiments have become massively dysfunctional, paralyzing the critical faculties of a large swath of the black intelligentsia. Indeed, as he sees it, the fear and loathing of betrayal that animates sellout rhetoric has paradoxically called into being the very trait such rhetoric seeks to combat. For the prospect of being labeled a race traitor has caused some blacks to suffer "a failure of nerve . . . that may be more accurately characterized as intellectual treason than racial fealty." After all, asks Loury, "what more important obligation can the privileged class of black elites have than to tell the truth to their own people?"[21]

There is another negative feature that is both a cause and a consequence of sellout rhetoric as it is typically deployed: recklessness in making hurtful allegations of racial disloyalty. Certain partisans of sellout vilification profess to be "serious about the drawing of political lines separating conduct that is merely disturbing or misguided from that which constitutes a conscious assault on African Americans as a people."[22] Little effort has been expended, however, in identifying criteria for the drawing of such lines. An article by Professor Martin Kilson suggested initially that it might address this omission. He entitled the article "How to Spot a 'Black Trojan Horse.'"[23] The "Black Trojan Horse" referred to is Cory Booker, a highly educated black politician who ran unsuccessfully for the mayoralty of Newark, New Jersey, in 2002 (but who won the election in 2006). Kilson sounded the alarm against Booker, describing him as a "New Wave" black conservative who was functioning "as an errand boy Black politician for conservative Republican power-class penetration of governing control of Black Newark." Kilson's denunciation of Booker for racial disloyalty was attended by virtually no description of Booker's proposed policies, much less any analysis of what it was about them that should be seen as objectionable. Largely prompting the indictment, it seems, was the character of some of Booker's supporters, including the conservative pundit George F. Will, who praised him in a column, and the conservative Manhattan Institute, at which Booker delivered an address. According to Kilson, "When you put together the appearance of George Will's celebratory column on Cory Booker and Booker's address at the Manhattan Institute the only conclusion to make . . . is that Booker is a 'Black Trojan Horse' for the rightwing." Again: at no point in his article does Kilson describe what Booker said in his speech at the Manhattan Institute or identify which policies endorsed by Booker gave him pause. Sometimes, in a pinch, when there is no time to investigate, one might have to act solely on the basis of crude signals that raise suspicion. (In other settings this practice is called profiling.) Kilson, however, faced no such emergency. Certainly before publicly accusing Cory Booker of being a black Trojan horse, the professor had time or should have made time to support his claim.

It would be a relief to say that this episode is unique. But that is simply not so. The character of Kilson's indictment—its vagueness, vituperativeness, dependence on innuendo—is all too common. Charges of a similar character surfaced in the Newark election itself, as the incumbent whom Booker challenged repeatedly insinuated that Booker's background—he is a graduate of Yale Law School—and his support from whites, including the editorial page of the *New York Times,* marked him as a turncoat. For a substantial number of black voters in Newark, the insinuations about white support were sufficient to cast a pall of suspicion over the challenger.[24]

Another problem with many deployments of sellout rhetoric involves determining what constitutes the best interest of blacks and the best means for achieving controversial goals. Many prosecutors of alleged sellouts proceed as if determining which policies best advance the interests of "the black community" is so easy that those who disagree with a supposed consensus are clearly either stupid, negligent, psychopathological, or traitorous. The sense that a person "knows (or ought to know) better" with respect to some given dispute is one of the things that encourages partisans of racial-betrayal rhetoric to label someone as a sellout. Hence, asserting that Colin Powell dispenses "political sweet poison," Reverend Al Sharpton maintains that "[t]here is no way that anyone who is that bright and that old could be so naïve about what the Republicans really stand for. He's got to know that he's selling something that is not in the interest of black people."[25] Similarly, those who condemn Clarence Thomas as a sellout often assert that he could not possibly believe what he says and that his votes can only sensibly be understood as the disingenuous acts of a turncoat who "knows better" but willfully proceeds in the wrong direction out of malevolence or for personal advantage. Many of Thomas's detractors simply fail to recognize that an appreciable number of blacks are genuinely conservative. This unwillingness or inability to acknowledge the ideological diversity of Black America homogenizes a population that has always been far more pluralistic than commonly acknowledged.

Homogenizing Black America's ideological diversity also tends to obscure the tragic dilemmas with which black people have grappled and which they continue to face. Was it commendable to defiantly confront slaveholders even at the cost of certain death? Or was a strategy of mere survival superior? Was it in the best interest of blacks to fight with the American revolutionaries in the War of Independence that gave rise to what became the United States of America? Or did the interest of blacks require fighting for the British? Was it in the best interest of blacks for antislavery activists to purchase runaway slaves and then emancipate them? Or did the interest of blacks demand an unyielding insistence that any and all transactions in slave markets be condemned as immoral? Whose approach to the challenge of Negrophobia was better—that of Booker T. Washington or that of W. E. B. DuBois? What was more commendable—Frederick Douglass's insistence that blacks stay in the United States and redeem it? Or Henry McNeal Turner's insistence that blacks should migrate to foreign soil where they could govern themselves without white domination? Was it in the best interest of blacks to serve in the armed forces of the United States even as that government segregated them and placed them under the guardianship of racist white officers? Or was the interest of blacks best advanced by making black participation conditional on equal treatment? Is racial integration the best goal or strategy for blacks? Or is inward-looking institution-building a preferable alternative?

Is it in the best interest of blacks for race to play a part in determining who should be permitted to adopt parentless children? Or is the best interest of blacks served by erasing race as a factor in adoptive proceedings? Do anti-gang loitering ordinances further the interests of the black community inasmuch as it tends to be disproportionately burdened by urban gang violence? Or are the interests of blacks predominantly served by rescinding or invalidating such measures? Is affirmative action in the best interest of the black community in that it virtually assures the presence of at least an appreciable number of Negroes in coveted, influential, strategic positions in American society? Or does affirmative action, on balance, hurt the black community by preempting more radical responses to social inequalities? Neither open nor veiled references to racial loyalty or disloyalty point the way toward reliable answers to such questions.*

How should black Americans proceed, given the problems that attend sellout rhetoric and its deployment?

One response is to repudiate racial sellout rhetoric in the course of repudiating the maintenance of racial solidarity. Those who embrace this position eschew efforts to create and maintain racial groups. They reject racial patriotism because they object to the idea that one ought to define one's obligations or commitments by reference to racial characteristics. They contend that no person should feel morally bound to express racial kinship with others who are deemed to be of the same race. They reject the notion that a person must or should join and assist the racial "team" to which society has assigned them by dint of skin color, hair type, nose width, and related indicia. Such persons repudiate the monitoring of racial boundaries because they oppose the maintenance of racially defined politics. They reject demands for racial

---

* "When Bill Cosby criticized blacks who he felt were hurting themselves and the community," Keith Boykin asks, "was that an act of loyalty or disloyalty? And when Michael Eric Dyson then criticized Bill Cosby for criticizing his community, was that an act of loyalty or disloyalty?" See Keith Boykin, "Condoleezza's Vice," keithboykin .com, Jan. 10, 2006.

loyalty because they oppose the existence of racial obligation in the first place. They decline to be "race men" or "race women" and opt instead to associate themselves with voluntary groupings that are free from the bounds of racial ascription.[26]*

This brand of cosmopolitanism occupies a marginal niche. Most blacks want to retain for the foreseeable future, if not permanently, a sense of group solidarity and its attendant manifestations in social, cultural, and political life (historically black colleges and universities, black student unions, black fraternities and sororities, black professional associations, etc.).

---

*This tradition, now at a low ebb, has a long history. In eighteenth-century America, there were some blacks, for instance, who objected to race-centered political organization or even to collective self-definition in terms of race. Hence, the black businessman-abolitionist William Whipper (1804–1876) objected to any "complexional"— that is to say, blacks only—organizations and urged African Americans to eschew labels that set them apart from other Americans. At the national black convention of 1835 he set forth a resolution (that passed!) that urged blacks to "abandon the use of the word 'colored,' when either speaking or writing concerning themselves; and especially to remove the title African from their institutions." He later explained: "We have too long witnessed the baneful effects of distinctions founded in hatred and prejudice, to advocate the insertion of either the word 'white' or 'colored.'" Whipper maintained that the label "oppressed Americans" was a better tool of self-perception and public presentation than any expressly racial label. Of like mind was the black journalist-abolitionist William Howard Day (1825–1900), who, in 1853, founded a newspaper in which he carefully avoided any sort of racial designation in the title. He called his paper the *Aliened American*. See Patrick Rael, *Black Identity and Black Protest in the Antebellum North* (2002), pp. 107–15.

A second response is to embrace black racial solidarity but to reject sellout rhetoric on the grounds that it is harming black communities. This is the position taken by Professors Carter and Loury, both of whom are avowed "race men." Previously I noted the individualistic slant of Carter's analysis—the priority he accords to the freedom of the intellectual and the encroachments on that freedom by peer pressure. But Carter is also concerned about the communal effects of demands for racial loyalty and concludes that those effects have been dismal. He maintains that, paradoxically, insistent calls for racial loyalty have had the consequence of undermining rather than encouraging a healthy racial unity. "Rather than bickering among ourselves," he writes, "we should be working together to fight the many real enemies that are crushing our people. . . . We need to avoid the error of thinking, however, that unity means solidarity and that solidarity, in turn, means groupthink; we have to delight in our diversity."[27] Elaborating upon the idea of delighting in African-American diversity, Carter envisions

> Thomas Sowell and Derrick Bell shaking hands across the conference table; Julius Lester and Jesse Jackson breaking bread together . . . not, perhaps, out of friendship but out of a deep and abiding mutual respect and a willingness to listen born of a shared love for our people and our troubled community.[28]

Carter also notes negative effects that are consistent with Loury's central theme that sellout rhetoric and its accompanying attitudes impoverish African-American thought by truncating needed debate. Carter maintains that African-American communities are losing valuable contributions from blacks who censor themselves because they are reluctant to offend those they see as their racial kin, because they believe that public intraracial disagreement is harmful, or because they are simply unwilling to risk the unloosing of aspersions upon their racial loyalty. Carter posits that black communities are being hurt by demands for racial loyalty insofar as some dissident blacks, unwilling to censor themselves, are essentially exiling themselves from Black America in order to express themselves fully. "[I]t makes no sense," Carter writes, "to alienate some of the best minds we have. . . . They dissent from the civil rights mainstream not because they do not care about the problem, but because they have thought about the problems and the traditional solutions alike; and thinking of better answers is something we should not discourage. . . . Our need for these free-thinking dissenters may prove to be greater than their need for us."[29]

To counteract what he views as dysfunctional peer-group pressure, Carter exhorts blacks to stop using or deferring to sellout rhetoric, to entertain fearlessly *any* ideas or argument, and to welcome within the big tent of blackness the full spectrum of beliefs and viewpoints held by African Americans. Arraying himself against the disciplinary authority of Soul Patrols, Carter maintains that blacks "must demand the right to comment on any subject, no matter how sacred to the orthodoxy."[30] Our task, he declares, is to build a reconciled solidarity "built not on our agreement on a program, not on our willingness to profess a particular viewpoint, but on our shared love of our people and our culture."[31] "There is more to racial solidarity and more to black pride," Carter insists, "than the effort to make everybody think the same way. Loving our people and loving our culture does not require any restriction on what black people can think or say or do or be."[32]

There is much that is attractive about Carter's position. It imaginatively seeks to embrace libertarianism on behalf of group advancement. At the same time, there are problems with this response. First and foremost, it fails to recognize a central sociological reality: collective action necessarily entails coercion or at least the threat of coercion. Every group confronts the task of curtailing free riding and defection. These tasks are key to any group's existence. Carter supports the continuation of blacks as a distinct community in American society. He also supports collective action on the part of blacks. Collective action, however, requires coordination, and coordination requires discipline, and discipline requires the punishment or threat of punishment that Carter finds so distressing. As professor of history Roger Wilkins notes, "Any community that thinks of itself as a community has drawn lines [and determined that] certain behavior puts you outside the community. For black Americans . . . it is legitimate to set parameters. In arguing how best we struggle, there is some political and intellectual behavior . . . that keeps you from being a black person."[33]

Carter and like-minded thinkers seem to reject the idea that an African American can ever properly be dismissed from the race—"de-blacked," to use Professor Kimberly Jade Norwood's vivid phrase.[34] How one stands on this matter will depend, at least in part, on how one conceptualizes "racial citizenship." If one views racial citizenship as an immutable status, then a person's association is fixed, beyond his or others' control. I do not, however, embrace that conception of racial citizenship. Instead, I embrace a conception in which choice is always an element of racial citizenship. In my view, all Negroes should be voluntary Negroes, blacks by choice, African Americans with a recognized right to resign from the race. By the same token, I see no reason why, in principle, an African American should not be subject to having his citizenship in Black America revoked if he chooses a course of conduct that convincingly demonstrates the absence of even a minimal communal allegiance.*

Carter is so appalled by the rhetorical violence that attends disputes among African Americans that he posits a program of pure tolerance, as when he writes, "Loving our people and loving our culture does not require any restriction on what black people can think or say or do

---

*American statutory and constitutional law allows for expatriation—revoking citizenship—but makes such revocation difficult to effectuate. The Supreme Court has held, for instance, that the federal constitution prohibits expatriation as a punishment for crime. See *Trop v. Dulles,* 356 U.S. 86 (1958). To expatriate an individual who has a legitimate claim to citizenship, the government must prove that the person specifically intended to renounce her citizenship. See *Vance v. Terrazas,* 444 U.S. 252 (1979).

or be."[35]* No restriction? But what about an African American who expresses racial dislike or even hatred for African Americans? What about an African American who joins a legitimate black uplift organization for the purpose of crippling its ability to advance the interests of black people? What about an African American who, though sincerely sympathetic to blacks, nonetheless views them as racial inferiors and urges that they be subjected to a wardship status by whites? That was the position taken by William Hannibal Thomas, who declared, you will recall, that blacks are "the waste product of American civilization."† Blacks banished Thomas, branding him a race traitor. They did not organize symposia to calmly weigh the upsides and downsides of his

---

*Similarly, Professor Kimberly Jade Norwood asserts that "there is no more important freedom than the freedom to think and to believe based upon personal conviction—no matter how unpopular that belief or conviction." ("The Virulence of Blackthink and How Its Threat of Ostracism Shackles Those Deemed Not Black Enough," 93 *Kentucky Law Journal* 144, 198 [2005].) But does one *really* want to embrace the proposition that "there is no more important freedom than the freedom to think and to believe based upon personal conviction"? What about the thought, the belief, the personal conviction that extermination is the proper destiny for certain peoples? I am willing to permit room for such thought as long as I am confident that circumstances doom it to impotent marginality. If belief in, say, Nazism had any plausible chance of growing, gaining adherents, and rising to power in this or any country, I would favor immediately crushing it. One can be against the imposition of "blackthink" and other stifling orthodoxies without embracing the proposition that *any* idea, no matter how brutal and dangerous, should, on principle, be immune from suppression.

†See pages 38–43.

proposal to separate black children from black parents. With virtual unanimity, they made him a pariah. Were they wrong to do so? I think not.

Carter and like-minded critics of "political correctness" speak as if ostracism, per se, is wrong. But that is mistaken. There is much ostracism that is *good*—ostracism of racists, misogynists, fascists, and purveyors of other hateful ideologies. We rightly describe as "progress" the successful repression of such ugly ideas and their attendant modes of conduct.

Carter appropriately praises the civil-rights revolution and previous efforts that have bettered conditions for black Americans. Racial monitoring and coercion were a part—an inevitable part—of each of these campaigns. Consider one of the most magnificent episodes of the civil-rights movement—the Montgomery Bus Boycott. In 1955, in response to egregious acts of racist mistreatment, prominent figures in the black community of Montgomery, Alabama (including Martin Luther King, Jr.), decided to boycott the city's buses in protest. The boycott was successful beyond all expectations. As a historian of the boycott observes:

> The boycott made black Montgomerians aware of themselves as a community with obligations and capacities to which they and others had previously been blind. On the eve of the boycott, few would have imagined the latent abilities that resided within that community. The protest elicited and clarified those abilities. On the eve of the boycott, few black Montgomerians would have considered themselves as persons with important political duties. The

protest inculcated and enlarged their sense of responsibility. Moreover, by publicizing their willingness and ability to mobilize united opposition to Jim Crow practices, the protesters in Montgomery contributed a therapeutic dose of inspiration to dissidents everywhere. Later developments would attest to the influence of the boycott as a role model that encouraged other acts of rebellion.[36]

The boycott is typically portrayed as an entirely voluntary enterprise in which the heroes of the story wage their struggle against racist villains without morally soiling their hands at all. The reality, however, was considerably more complicated. The boycott was mainly animated by the commitment of many blacks to reform, if not erase, patterns of racial subordination that they rightly abhorred. It is important to note, however, that the boycott was also reinforced by the knowledge that any black person caught riding the buses would face ostracism from his peers. He or she would be denounced as a sellout—or words to that effect. That the fear of reprisal acted as a coercive influence is no mere speculation. A number of blacks who sought to ride despite the boycott testified in court proceedings that they were physically harassed or intimidated by supporters of the strike. As it turns out, extraordinarily few African Americans rode the buses. More would have evaded the boycott, however, had they not feared the cost of attempting to do so. This sliver of black Montgomery would have included Negroes who either opposed the boycott on ideological grounds or opposed being enlisted in a strike by which they did not want to be inconvenienced. These blacks have largely been airbrushed from the public memory of the boycott. But they did exist and should be taken into account.

Sellout rhetoric and its concomitant attitudes, gestures, and strategies can prompt excessive self-censorship, truncate needed debate, and nurture demagoguery. But ostracism, or at least the potential for ostracism, is also part of the unavoidable cost of collective action and group maintenance. Thus, to the extent that Carter and his camp want to perpetuate black communities but eschew any internal monitoring of these communities, they want a sociological impossibility. The identification and stigmatization of taboos, including betrayal, are simply inescapable, albeit dangerous, aspects of any collective enterprise.

Racial solidarity among African Americans will always depend to some extent on those whom Professor Loury derisively describes as "self-appointed guardians of racial virtue."[37] Loury and Carter are themselves such guardians. Their chiding of black political correctness is itself an effort to police the boundaries of "good" racial conduct within Black America. In his polite fashion, Carter seeks to place out of bounds blacks who try to put other blacks out of bounds. Loury does the same thing, but more overtly and with a wider sweep. For he urges ostracizing not only those who routinely label black adversaries as sellouts; he also urges ostracizing blacks who permit themselves to be intimidated into silence. Their reticence, Loury declares, "represents a failure of nerve . . . that may be more accurately characterized as intellectual treason than racial fealty."[38] What could be a clearer example than this of racial guardianship?

In the end, those who want to maintain black solidarity but contain the dysfunctional aspects of the peer pressure that makes effective collective action possible must recognize that solidarity always poses a problem of balance between collective unity and individual freedom. Acknowledgment of this dilemma will facilitate healthy rejection of both the indifference to pluralism displayed by impatient devotees of sellout rhetoric and the indifference to group discipline displayed by those who reject out of hand any efforts by blacks to ostracize free riders and defectors in their ranks. If a group exists, there must be some conduct in which a member can engage that is appropriately labeled "betrayal." For the proponent of black solidarity, therefore, the best response to excessive sellout rhetoric is a limited response that attempts to regulate rather than abolish that rhetoric.* This response should inject more thoughtfulness into the discussion over racial betrayal by holding accountable not only suspects but also accusers: anyone who indicts another for selling out should be held responsible for the accusation. If it is found to be unwarranted, the accuser should be made to feel at least some of the pain that his or her accusation has wrongly inflicted upon an undeserving target. By examining accusations with more care and raising the

---

*An example of what I have in mind here is the excellent book by Tommie Shelby, *We Who Are Dark: The Philosophical Foundations of Black Solidarity* (2005).

prospect that errant accusers will find themselves sub-jected to ostracism, sellout rhetoric will hopefully become less pervasive and more disciplined, less a weapon of demagoguery and more an allegation that protagonists and onlookers alike regard gravely.

Four

THE CASE OF CLARENCE THOMAS[1]

> "*He is an enemy of our race . . . [T]he fact that Thomas is a brother should make us hold him to an even higher standard, not provide him with a way to weasel out of taking responsibility for being a traitor.*"
>
> Pearl Cleage, *Deals with the Devil and Other Reasons to Riot* (1993)

"I hope [Clarence Thomas's] wife feeds him lots of eggs and butter, and he dies early like many black men do of heart disease," Julianne Malveaux declared in a televised panel discussion. "He's an absolutely reprehensible person."[2] Expressing a similarly hostile view, a newspaper columnist urged his readers "to just chill and pray that one day the dreaded Uncle Thomas Reptilious will be extinct."[3] That animosity toward Justice Clarence Thomas would prompt prayers for his death should be no surprise given the offense he is charged with committing: supporting the enemies of black folk, subverting Black America, being a race traitor. That is why Thomas is the most vilified black official in the history of the

United States. His name has become synonymous with selling out. To "pull a Clarence Thomas" is to engage in racial betrayal.* Imploring the Senate to block Thomas's elevation to the Supreme Court, Congressman Major Owens asked his colleagues to "try to imagine how the French would have felt if the collaborator Marshal Pétain had been awarded a medal after the liberation of France in World War II, or if in Norway Quisling had been made a high official in the government," or if, after the War for Independence, Benedict Arnold had been promoted to the level of a general.[4]

Subsequent to his confirmation, Thomas has continued to be the target of constant denunciation. Indicative of the animosity he often faces is an incident that arose in Savannah, Georgia, in 2001. A white businessman, Harlan Crow, approached a local foundation that was involved in renovating a library—the formerly segregated library that Thomas had used as a child. Crow offered to donate money to complete the renovation on the condition that the library be renamed in honor of Thomas. Several black members of the agency overseeing the project objected, with one declaring, "Clarence Thomas has never cared anything about black folks. . . . I call him Judas because he sold his people out."[5]

---

*See *The Early Show* CBS News transcript, May 16, 2007 (Russ Mitchell remarks that "In the black community to be called a Clarence Thomas [is to be] considered someone who sells out"); Steven Heller, *Design Dialogues* (1998) (insinuating that the artist Michael Ray Charles is a sellout, a critic asks the artist, "How does it feel to be the Clarence Thomas of the art world?").

A former president of the Madison, Wisconsin, NAACP derided Thomas as a charter member of the "Sell-Out Hall of Shame."[6] A civil-rights activist in Memphis, Tennessee, Reverend Billy Kyles, protested Thomas's appearance at a bar association meeting by carrying a sign that read "Uncle Thomas: Why Do You Burn the Bridges That Brought You Over?"[7] A black-owned media network, the Northeastern Network, facetiously awarded Thomas its Buckwheat Award, describing it as "a special recognition for Blacks who excel in minstrelsy."[8] Thomas is becoming "to the Black community," Reverend Joseph Lowery declared, "what Benedict Arnold was to the nation he deserted; and what Judas Iscariot was to Jesus: a traitor, and what Brutus was to Caesar: an assassin."[9] Eric Ferrer, a black member of the board of the Civil Liberties Union of Hawaii, resigned his seat when his colleagues merely considered inviting Justice Thomas to participate in a debate on affirmative action. Inviting Thomas, Ferrer complained, would be similar to "inviting Hitler to come speak on the rights of Jews."[10] According to Wiley Hall of the *Baltimore Evening Sun*, "Uncle Thomas deliberately feeds society's stereotypes about blacks and he does so for his personal gain." He "denigrates the hard work, sacrifice and struggle of his own people." He commits the crime of "reassuring racists."[11] Derrick Z. Jackson of the *Boston Globe* accused Thomas of participating in "drive-by shootings of black progress."[12] The butt of countless jokes—"Perhaps black people ought to give serious thought to retiring 'Clarence' from general use as a name

in our communities"[13]—Thomas has also been the focus
of a popular rapper's ire. According to KRS-One:

> The white man ain't the devil, I promise.   ·
> You want to see the devil, take a look at Clarence
>   Thomas.[14]

Those who accuse Thomas of racial betrayal do not
delineate in detail the elements of the offense they charge
him with committing. One can infer from their accusations, however, that they mean to convict him of something much more blameworthy than being wrong, or
even terribly wrong, about a disputed public policy. They
mean to convict him in the court of public opinion for
intentionally undermining African-American communal
well-being or for utter indifference to the collective interest of blacks. Thus one hears accusers say of him that "as
a black man he knows better or should know better"
than to say what he says, believe what he believes, conclude what he concludes. It is this sense that Thomas
and all "sellouts" know better or should know better
that prompts their accusers to view them as social criminals who are acting outside the bounds within which reasonable people can reasonably disagree.

Thomas did not begin his association with the
Supreme Court as a pervasively scorned figure in Black
America. When he was nominated by President George
H. W. Bush to fill the seat vacated by Thurgood Marshall
in 1991, polling revealed that 54 percent of African
Americans approved of his nomination while 17 percent
disapproved. After his nomination was imperiled by his

former assistant Anita Hill's allegations that he sexually harassed her, his support among blacks jumped considerably, with one poll showing a rise in support to 63 percent while another showed a rise to 70 percent. Five years later, after constant disparagement by civil-rights activists, ministers, journalists, entertainers, teachers, politicians, and other influential arbiters of opinion in Black America, a poll conducted by the Joint Center for Political and Economic Studies indicated that 44 percent of blacks had an unfavorable view of Thomas and only 32 percent viewed him favorably.

In a poll conducted in December 2000 (in the immediate aftermath of the Bush-Gore election struggle and the Supreme Court's controversial resolution of it), 52 percent of blacks (but only 30 percent of whites) stated that they had an unfavorable opinion of Thomas, while 35 percent of blacks (and 49 percent of whites) stated that they had a favorable opinion of the justice.[15] The large number of blacks who now express antipathy toward Thomas may not know precisely what there is about his beliefs or votes that they dislike. But they have been told repeatedly and insistently by people they trust that they ought to abhor Thomas—advice that has been widely followed.

Leading shapers of black public opinion fervently discredit Thomas, for a variety of reasons. One is the "pulling up the ladder" (or "burning the bridge") critique. Detractors argue that, having climbed the affirmative-action ladder himself, it is unbecoming for Thomas to seek now to remove it from the grasp of fellow blacks.

Urging the Senate to reject Thomas's appointment to the Supreme Court, Congressman John Lewis told his colleagues, "What you have is a nominee who wants to destroy the bridge that brought him over troubled waters."[16] Congressman Louis Stokes voiced the same sentiment:

> The difference between Judge Thomas and most black Americans who have achieved, in spite of poverty, adversity, and racism is that most of them have not forgotten from whence they have come. Whenever possible, they have used their educations and positions of achievement to help eliminate from our society these barriers to equal opportunity, liberty, and justice. It is almost unheard of to see them utilize their educations and positions to impede the progress of those less fortunate than they."[17]

The writer Rosemary Bray averred that Thomas had "gradually revealed himself to be a man who rejoiced in burning the bridges that brought him over."* According to NAACP official John Odom, "Thomas crosses bridges built by others, torches them and pretends that bridges are unnecessary, that those on the other side are simply too lazy to swim."[18] In response to a Thomas opinion

---

*Bray also noted that for her the confirmation hearings of Clarence Thomas took on the character of a dreaded nightmare. "The particular dread I felt was one of betrayal—not a betrayal by President Bush, from whom I expected nothing—but by Thomas himself." See Rosemary L. Bray, "Taking Sides Against Ourselves" in *Court of Appeal: The Black Community Speaks Out on the Racial and Sexual Politics of* Thomas v. Hill, Robert Chrisman and Robert L. Allen, eds. (1992), p. 47.

attacking the legitimacy of an affirmative-action program at the University of Michigan, the *New York Times* columnist Maureen Dowd echoed the same theme. "It's impossible," she asserted, "not to be disgusted [by] someone who could benefit so much from affirmative action and then pull the ladder up after himself."[19]

Nothing has been more central to the vilification of Clarence Thomas than his opposition to racial affirmative action—programs that expressly benefit racial minorities in competition for scarce, highly coveted positions in employment or educational institutions. Were he to have taken a different position on *that* issue, his relationship to other African Americans would be altogether different, because affirmative action has emerged over the past thirty years as *the* key defining racial issue among most politically active, ideologically self-aware, and well-organized African Americans. Strongly supportive of affirmative action are the major black pressure groups, many of the most influential figures in Black America, and the African Americans who express their preferences most intensely regarding this matter.* For many in this

---

*Illustrative of this fact is the stark difference in the racial demographics of those who submit friends of the court briefs in key judicial cases. In the landmark 2003 cases involving the University of Michigan, there is only a spectral black presence among the opponents to affirmative action. By contrast, black proponents are numerous and visible, as indicated by amicus curiae briefs submitted on behalf of the United Negro College Fund, the NAACP Legal Defense Fund, the National Urban League, the New York State Black and Puerto Rican Legislative Caucus, black student and professional organizations (for example, the Harvard Black Law Students Association),

camp, to be against affirmative action is tantamount to being antiblack. Contrary views on gay rights, environmental policy, abortion, tax policy, foreign affairs, or church-state relations are acceptable. But contrary opinion on affirmative action is unacceptable. It is the litmus test. In the early 1980s, when I was a student at Yale Law School, a substantial number of black students took the position that opposition to affirmative action was illegitimate and that they would leave class if debate on the subject arose, because the existence of black students at the school was nondebatable and nonnegotiable. A decade later, in *Reflections of an Affirmative Action Baby*, Stephen Carter observed (disapprovingly) that among elite blacks, affirmative action had become a shibboleth looked to as a basis for distinguishing friends from enemies.[20] "Among the black middle class," observes Orlando Patterson, "especially on the nation's campuses, blind support for affirmative action has become an essential signal of ethnic solidarity."[21] President Clinton attained a deep and wide popularity with black Americans that did not suffer substantially even when he adopted certain positions adverse to those held by most black politicians, such as his refusal to soften draconian penalties for drug offenses that disproportionately fall upon blacks by a dramatic margin. Yet even Bill

---

and several ad hoc associations (for example, the Committee of Concerned Black Graduates of ABA Accredited Law Schools). See *Gratz v. Bollinger,* 539 U.S. 244, 248–51 (2003); *Grutter v. Bollinger,* 539 U.S. 306, 310–14 (2003).

Clinton declined to touch the third rail of Black American politics, finessing the affirmative-action issue with his clever "mend it, don't end it" formulation.[22] One of the reasons Colin Powell has retained his high standing among blacks despite his close associations with the Reagan and Bush administrations—regimes notoriously unpopular among African Americans—is that, whatever other positions he adopted, Powell never repudiated affirmative action.[23]

Thomas followed a different path. As an official in the Reagan administration, he spoke out vociferously against affirmative action (or, in the lingo of conservatives, "preferential treatment"). As chairman of the Equal Employment Opportunity Commission (EEOC) he wrote, "I firmly insist that the Constitution be interpreted in a colorblind fashion. It is futile to talk of a colorblind society unless this constitutional principle is first established. Hence, I emphasize black self-help, as opposed to racial quotas and other race-conscious legal devices that only further and deepen the original problem."[24] Moreover, he openly criticized Supreme Court decisions that upheld affirmative-action programs, stating among other things that the Court had "reinterpret[ed] civil rights laws to create schemes of racial preference where none was ever contemplated."[25]

At the time of his Supreme Court confirmation hearings, some black observers refused to accept that Thomas's preconfirmation statements represented what he really believed or would come to embrace as a justice. Some blacks thought that his harsh anti–affirmative action rhetoric was part of a ruse he deemed momentarily necessary to "get over," a charade he would end once he ascended to the Supreme Court with the security of life tenure. A skit on the television comedy show *In Living Color* displayed this view. In the skit, Thomas is portrayed initially as a servile figure, eagerly doing menial chores for the white justices. After one of them tells Thomas that he is protected by life tenure, he abruptly changes his demeanor. He kicks off his shoes, puts his feet up on a table, and starts to speak in an identifiably "black" fashion. This skit, observes Professor Melissa Victoria Harris-Lacewell, "was expressing the hope of black Americans that Thomas would turn out to be a trickster who had spent all those years fooling whites until he got into a position of power."[26]

Other blacks thought that even if Thomas's statements were sincere, he would mellow due to the cumulative weight of his racial experiences, a latent sense of racial solidarity, and a heightened sense of political responsibility. The poet Maya Angelou wrote in favor of Thomas's confirmation on precisely this ground. She supported him, she wrote, "because Clarence Thomas has been poor, has been nearly suffocated by the acrid odor of racial discrimination, is intelligent, well-trained, black and young enough to be won over again."[27]

As a justice, however, Thomas has been unremittingly hostile to affirmative action. Indeed, no justice is more antagonistic.

Thomas's jurisprudence articulates two main points. First, as a matter of federal constitutional law, he maintains that *all* racial distinctions are presumptively illicit regardless of the motivations of their authors. "As far as the Constitution is concerned," he writes, "it is irrelevant whether a government's racial classifications are drawn by those who wish to oppress a race or by those who have a sincere desire to help those thought to be disadvantaged."[28] In Thomas's view, there is (or should be) no constitutional difference between positive (i.e., remedial or diversity-based) racial distinctions and negative (i.e., white supremacist or separatist) racial distinctions. "[T]here is a moral [and] constitutional equivalence," he contends, "between laws designed to subjugate a race and those that distribute benefits on the basis of race in order to foster some current notion of equality.... [G]overnment-sponsored racial discrimination based on benign prejudice is just as noxious as discrimination inspired by malicious prejudice. In each instance, it is racial discrimination, plain and simple."[29]

Thomas does not go so far as to say that governmental racial distinctions are *always* illegal. Rather he maintains that all public racial distinctions should be subject to judicial "strict scrutiny." To Thomas, subjecting a racial distinction to strict scrutiny means viewing it as presumptively illegal and upholding it only for the exceptional purpose of meeting a "pressing public necessity" by narrowly tailored means.* In Thomas's view, the pur-

---

*In 2005 the Supreme Court adjudicated a challenge to a state policy that segregated prisoners by race each time they entered a new facility. The claimed purpose of the policy was to minimize or prevent violence. The Court held that the policy, insofar as it made racial

pose of racial affirmative-action programs is insuffi-
ciently weighty and the design of such programs is insuf-
ficiently tailored to satisfy his standard of strict scrutiny.

Second, as a matter of policy, Thomas disparages affirmative action as a counterproductive form of "racial
paternalism" that harms its purported beneficiaries—a
point on which I will elaborate below—as well as the collective soul of the nation. "Every time the government
places citizens on racial registers and makes race relevant
to the provision of burdens or benefits, it demeans us
all."[30] Moreover, Thomas warns, even assuming that the
authors of affirmative-action programs harbor laudable
motives, the "unintended consequences [of the pro-
grams] can be as poisonous and pernicious as any other
form of discrimination. So-called 'benign' discrimination
teaches many that because of chronic and apparently
immutable handicaps, minorities cannot compete with
them without their patronizing indulgence. Inevitably,
such programs engender attitudes of superiority or, alter-
natively, provoke resentment among those who believe

---

distinctions, should be assessed using "strict scrutiny." Justice
Thomas dissented, maintaining that in the context of regulating prisons, conventional constitutional limitation on state officials should be
relaxed. A color-blind absolutist in the affirmative action context,
here Thomas decided that flexibility is warranted. "The Constitution
has always demanded less within the prison walls," Thomas declared.
"Time and again, even when faced with constitutional rights no less
'fundamental' than the right to be free from state-sponsored racial
discrimination, we have deferred to the reasonable judgments of officials experienced in running this Nation's prisons." *Johnson v. California,* 543 U.S. 499, 524 (2005).

that they have been wronged by the government's use of race. These programs stamp minorities with a badge of inferiority and may cause them to develop dependencies or to adopt an attitude that they are 'entitled' to preferences."[31]

To Thomas, affirmative action not only stigmatizes in the long term *all* members of the "beneficiary" group—including those who would have prevailed in the absence of a racial preference—it also often fails in the short term to assist those racial minorities most in need of assistance. Excoriating affirmative action in law-school admissions, Thomas complains that "racial discrimination" at such institutions "does nothing for those too poor or uneducated to participate in elite higher education and therefore presents only an illusory solution to the challenges facing our Nation."[32] Attacking affirmative action with a rhetoric and logic typically associated with commentators situated on the political left,[33] Thomas denounces it as a failed effort undertaken primarily by two self-interested parties. The first are white elites who seek on the cheap to achieve the appearance of racial equality by preferring the window dressing of affirmative action or "diversity" to more radical measures. The second are black elites who feed off a bounty generated by white guilt that is largely inaccessible to ghettoized urban blacks or impoverished rural blacks.

What should one make of Thomas's attack on affirmative action? It is deeply flawed. Its vulnerabilities, however, have often been obscured by misleading arguments voiced by some of the justice's most influential detractors. One such argument is that Thomas's rejection of affirmative action is illegitimate, since he benefited from it. For example, Judge A. Leon Higginbotham, Jr., posed the following as a rhetorical question:

> Under what rationale does Justice Clarence Thomas, [after having enjoyed the affirmative action] that made his success possible, have the moral basis to become hostile to such options being made available to the present generation of African Americans, many of whom have found barriers to entry as high and impenetrable as any he encountered?[34]

Whether an official ought to tolerate or support a policy, however, should be dependent on other-regarding considerations ("Is this policy just, effective, prudent?" etc.), not self-regarding considerations ("Does this policy help you or your people?"). Surely, it would be improper to criticize a white jurist for condemning Jim Crow segregation simply because he had previously benefited from it. Being a beneficiary of a policy should not disable one from repudiating it. If it is a bad policy it should be rejected even (or perhaps especially) by its beneficiaries.

Thomas vehemently denies that he has been a beneficiary of affirmative action.[35] His denials provoke his detractors all the more. They point out that the available evidence indicates overwhelmingly that Thomas benefited greatly from decision-makers' positive consideration of his race for purposes of admission to law school and for subsequent political appointments, including his nomination to the Supreme Court.[36] President Bush asserted that Thomas's race had had nothing to do with his nomination. But that claim is risible;[37] it was by no means accidental that Justice Thomas was tapped to replace the only black member of the Court. Still, what should be determinative in assessing Thomas's rulings on affirmative action is not whether that policy assisted him, but whether it is statutorily or constitutionally legitimate.[38]

Instead of denouncing Thomas's objection to affirmative action on grounds of racial disloyalty, personal ingratitude, or hypocrisy, proponents of affirmative action should explain how, on legal and moral grounds, he is wrong. A useful start could focus on Justice Thomas's reverential invocation of Justice John Marshall Harlan's statement that "our Constitution is color blind."[39] "My view of the Constitution," Thomas asserts, "is Justice Harlan's view in *Plessy*."[40] Offered in his dissenting opinion in *Plessy v. Ferguson*,[41] Harlan's declaration bracingly challenged the Supreme Court's complacent affirmance of *de jure* segregation on intrastate railway transportation.* Note, though, that no reference to color

---

*It should be recognized, however, that Harlan was no racial egalitarian. Though he argued that, in his view, the Constitution prohibits states from discriminating against blacks, he also made plain his belief that whites are, in fact, superior to blacks. Moreover, he voted with majorities in decisions that helped solidify the legal framework of Jim Crow segregation. See *Pace v. Alabama*, 106 U.S. 583 (1883) (upholding a statute that penalized interracial fornication more harshly than intraracial fornication); *Cumming v. Richmond County Board of Education*, 175 U.S. 528 (1899) (upholding a decision of school board to end access to public secondary education for blacks while retaining access to public secondary education for whites). With respect to the Chinese, Harlan was racist to the core. In the same *Plessy* dissent for

blindness is found on the face of the Constitution. The great abolitionist Wendell Phillips proposed a Fourteenth Amendment that would have forbidden public authorities expressly and categorically from making any racial distinctions. Phillips's proposed amendment read:

> No state shall make any distinction in civil rights and privileges . . . on account of race, color, or descent.[42]

But Congress explicitly rejected that proposal and instead promulgated a provision that enjoins states to offer to all persons the "equal protection of the laws"—a standard that is famously ambiguous and malleable.

In several areas of constitutional law, Thomas couches his opinions in an originalist framework, seemingly devoted to determining how the constitutional provision at hand was originally understood by its framers. He has explicitly maintained that he is committed to interpreting the Constitution not according to his own preferences, but according to the expressed preferences of those who authored and ratified the texts in question. As Thomas puts it:

---

which he is often lavishly praised, Justice Harlan declared approvingly, referring to the Chinese, that "there is a race so different from our own that we do not permit those belonging to it to become citizens of the United States." 163 U.S. 561. He also joined in promulgating several Supreme Court decisions that egregiously diminished the legal status of the Chinese. See Gabriel J. Chin, "The Plessy Myth: Justice Harlan and the Chinese Cases," 82 *Iowa Law Review* 151 (1996).

> When interpreting the Constitution and statutes, judges
> should seek the original understanding of the provision's
> text if the meaning of that text is not readily apparent. . . .
> The Constitution means what the delegates of the Philadel-
> phia Convention and the State ratifying conventions under-
> stood it to mean, not what we judges think it should
> mean.[43]

He alludes to the need for self-discipline as a principal
reason for proceeding as an originalist. That approach,
he asserts, "works in several ways to reduce judicial dis-
cretion and to maintain judicial impartiality. . . . By teth-
ering their analysis to the understanding of those who
drafted and ratified the text, modern judges are prevented from substituting their own preferences for the
Constitution."[44]

In the context of affirmative action, however, Thomas
shows little interest in examining the intentions of the
framers of the Fourteenth Amendment.[45] Perhaps that
has something to do with the fact that the historical
record shows that the framers and ratifiers of the Fourteenth Amendment did not intend to establish a "color
blind" regime. In 1866, the Congress that framed the
Fourteenth Amendment subsequently enacted a statute
appropriating money for "the relief of colored women
and children." The next year, the Congress that ensured
the ratification of the Fourteenth Amendment enacted a
statute providing relief for destitute "colored" people in
the District of Columbia. "Year after year in the Civil
War period—before, during, and after ratification of the
Fourteenth Amendment—Congress made special appro-

priations for awarding bounty and prize money to the 'colored' soldiers and sailors in the Union Army."[46]*

Race-baiting opponents of the Fourteenth Amendment sometimes suggested that it would bring about— horror, horror!—the end of all racial distinctions. They

---

*In *Parents Involved in Community Schools v. Seattle School District No. 1 et al.*, in which the Supreme Court invalidated a student assignment plan that used racial distinctions to maintain racial diversity in public high schools, Justice Thomas briefly responded to originalist arguments in favor of racial distinctions aimed at assisting blacks. He maintained that race-based government measures during the 1860s and 1870s to remedy state-enforced slavery were not inconsistent with his conception of constitutional limitations, since "the color-blind Constitution does not bar the government from taking measures to remedy state-sponsored discrimination" (127 S. Ct 2782 n. 19). But the laws that the Congress passed that expressly targeted "colored" beneficiaries were not enacted as remedies for racial discrimination; they constituted emergency, humanitarian relief.

Although Thomas is silent on the issue, it could be argued that the Equal Protection Clause of the Fourteenth Amendment of the Constitution limits only the states and not the federal government. See Paul Brest, Sanford Levinson, Jack M. Balkin, Akhil Reed Amar, and Reva B. Siegel, *Processes of Constitutional Decisionmaking: Cases and Materials* (fifth edition, 2006), pp. 1116–17. If that is so, however, then what limits the federal government from imposing racial discriminations? Justice Thomas has joined the Court in declaring that, in terms of race policy, the Fifth Amendment of the Constitution limits the federal government to the same extent that the Fourteenth Amendment limits the states. See *Adarand Constructors v. Pena*, 515 U.S. 200 (1995). Yet the Fifth Amendment, too, poses a problem for originalists. After all, it became part of the Constitution in 1791, when all manner of invidious racial discriminations, including racial slavery, were common and widely accepted. The framers and ratifiers of the Fifth Amendment certainly did not intend to bar the United States from imposing racial exclusions such as the statute that long

especially liked raising this specter in the context of discussing state laws that prohibited marriage across racial lines. Because such laws were popular, opponents of the Fourteenth Amendment believed that they could arouse widespread grass-roots opposition by invoking the threat of racial amalgamation, which was, to whites, a much feared and hated prospect. The response by champions of the Fourteenth Amendment is instructive. They replied that it would not require the abolition of laws prohibiting racial intermarriage because the Fourteenth Amendment demanded not the cessation of racial distinctions but only neutrality with respect to the imposition of such restrictions. Whites and blacks could be barred from marrying one another as long as the prohibition, in form, burdened whites and blacks equally.[47] That Thomas avoids grappling with this historical reality should not be surprising; it poses a major problem for originalists—a problem that Thomas is content to overlook. This evasion supports Professor André Cummings's observation that Thomas "abandons his originalist jurisprudential philosophy whenever it fits his political [agenda to do so]."[48]

Thomas asserts that the Constitution requires an

---

limited eligibility for naturalization to whites only. The conservative jurist Robert H. Bork acknowledges that under originalist premises the Fifth Amendment cannot properly be judged as having prohibited the federal government from enacting racial distinctions. See *The Tempting of America* (1997), pp. 83–84. Justice Thomas, by contrast, quietly ducks the difficulties posed by this subject while loudly repeating his favorite mantras.

absence of racial distinctions—except in certain defined circumstances. His reference to "the Constitution" makes it seem as though some external force issues directives that Thomas, as a justice, merely obeys. But the constitutional text mentions neither "color blindness" nor "strict scrutiny" nor any of the other doctrines that judges have designed to effectuate the Constitution in practice.[49] Contrary to the impression that Thomas advances, judging—especially constitutional adjudication at the Supreme Court—is an inescapably policy-making enterprise. The rulings Thomas makes involve exercises in choice for which he personally can and should be held responsible.[50]

Contrary to what Thomas maintains, there is nothing in the federal Constitution that requires repudiating affirmative action. The constitutional text does not expressly or even implicitly forbid policies aimed at specifically assisting racial minorities that have been purposefully oppressed for long periods by governmental and nongovernmental actors. The framers of the Fourteenth Amendment (and their constituents) did not intend to ban all government-endorsed racial distinctions; they supported what they viewed as race-neutral antimiscegenation laws and other segregation policies and supported as well laws that expressly singled out African Americans for special assistance. Furthermore, a sensible understanding of constitutional equality could certainly accommodate affirmative action by interpreting the Fourteenth Amendment as a device protecting groups against *unfriendly* racial legislation—not against *friendly* efforts to assist groups in overcoming legacies of racial subjugation.*

A strong argument could be made that judicial intervention against affirmative action would be warranted if there existed no political accountability for affirmative action or if affirmative action discriminated in favor of those who had effective control over it. But as Professor John Hart Ely noted long ago (in an excellent article that failed, unfortunately, to gain much influence outside of legal academia), affirmative action in the United States typically involves programs of assistance to racial minorities that are under the effective control of white majori-

---

Strauder v. West Virginia, 100 U.S. 303 (1880), marked the first time the Supreme Court applied the Fourteenth Amendment in a racial context. Seeking to pour specificity into the amendment's elliptical pronouncement, the Court maintained that the new provision contained "a necessary implication of a positive immunity, or right, most valuable to the colored race—the right of exemption from unfriendly legislation against them distinctively as colored—exemption from legal discriminations, implying inferiority in civil society, lessening the security of their enjoyment of the rights which others enjoy, and discriminations which are steps towards reducing them to the condition of a subject race." Id., p. 308. Affirmative action for blacks is consonant with *Strauder* in that it is not a legal discrimination "against" blacks. Justice Thomas, however, would dispute that empirical claim; he does view affirmative action as a legal discrimination that implies the inferiority of blacks in civil society. It must be noted, moreover, that elsewhere in *Strauder* the Court maintains that the Equal Protection Clause of the Fourteenth Amendment stands for the proposition that "the law in the States shall be the same for the black as for the white." Id., p. 307. A requirement of sameness in the law might well preclude affirmative action. For bringing my attention to the significance and richness of *Strauder* I thank my beloved teacher and mentor, Professor Sanford Levinson.

ties.[51] Under those circumstances, regular electoral politics can be trusted to discipline affirmative action (as has
happened in California and Michigan, where plebiscites
have abolished the practice).

Whether governments (or private entities) *ought* to
establish or continue affirmative-action programs is a
much closer question. On the one hand, affirmative
action has strikingly benefited blacks as a group and the
nation as a whole. It has enabled blacks to attain occupational and educational advancement in numbers and at a
pace that would otherwise have been impossible. These
breakthroughs engender self-perpetuating benefits: the
accumulation of valuable experience, the expansion of a
professional class able to pass its material advantages
and elevated aspirations to subsequent generations, the
rebutting of debilitating stereotypes, and the inclusion of
black participants in consequential decision-making.
Without affirmative action, access for black applicants to
elite positions would be considerably narrowed.

Furthermore, the benefits of affirmative action redound
not only to blacks but to the nation as a whole. Recall
that the virtual absence of black police officers even in
overwhelmingly black areas helped spark the ghetto
rebellions of the 1960s. The racial integration of police
forces through strong affirmative-action measures has
often led to better relations between minority communities and the police, a result that improves public safety for
all. Positive externalities have accompanied affirmative-
action programs in other contexts as well, most notably
the armed forces, by bringing into fruitful contact diverse

perspectives that are too often isolated and by teaching everyone that blacks, too, are capable of handling responsibility, dispensing knowledge, and applying valued skills.

On the other hand, Justice Thomas offers in opposition arguments that have been voiced by a wide range of intelligent observers. These commentators have argued that affirmative action entrenches the idea that blacks are unalterably inferior to whites; that it puts a pall over the achievements of all blacks (whether or not they received a boost from an affirmative-action program);* that it assists those who are relatively privileged while providing little or no assistance to those most in need of help; that it nourishes a visceral resentment among whites that prompts large numbers of them to oppose not only affirmative action but other policies widely perceived as helpful to racial minorities; that affirmative action has taken up far too much limited political space, thereby marginalizing other concerns; that it reinforces the status quo by deflecting attention from the root causes of disparities in educational and occupational achievement; that affirma-

---

*Speaking to this issue in the context of law-school admissions, Justice Thomas writes:

> The majority of blacks are admitted to the [University of Michigan] Law School because of discrimination, and because of this policy all are tarred as undeserving. . . . When blacks take positions in the highest places of government, industry, or academia, it is an open question today whether their skin color played a role in their advancement. The question itself is a stigma.

Grutter v. Bollinger, 539 U.S., 373.

tive action is defended dishonestly in terms of "diversity" when in fact the real basis for the program is reparations; that it has contributed to the demobilization of Black America by buying off Negro elites and confusing the African-American masses.

These are weighty objections that warrant close attention. But these objections should be assessed in a realistic context that asks whether American society is marginally better off with affirmative action (despite its drawbacks) or marginally better off without affirmative action (despite its benefits). I conclude that the former is more likely, given the limited set of plausible alternatives. I readily concede, however, that there is ample evidence for a reasonable conclusion that goes the other way. I disagree with that conclusion. But judgments the other way are surely understandable.

A notable feature of Thomas's participation in the debate over affirmative action is that he concedes virtually nothing to those with whom he disagrees. He acknowledges no significant public benefit bestowed by affirmative action. He portrays it as one big cynical misbegotten ruse. In this sense he mirrors many of his harshest detractors. Like them, he ignores or is blind to good points made by ideological opponents.

Justice Thomas is fond of lecturing others about the virtues of civility and the dangers of assuming bad faith on the part of those with whom one disagrees.[52] In one speech he insists: "People with whom you disagree have a point of view that you should respect or at least listen to." In another he states: "I go to great lengths to go after the ideas and never the person [with whom I disagree]."[53] Actually, however, Thomas is prone to disparaging the motives of those with whom he differs. In criticizing the authorities at the University of Michigan Law School for their affirmative-action program, it was not enough for Justice Thomas to assert that, in his view, they were advancing policies that were unwise and unconstitutional. He also asserted that they were deceitful, manipulative, and ultimately unconcerned about contributing to the achievement of a higher measure of social justice. "[A]ll the Law School cares about," Thomas charges, "is its own image among know-it-all elites, not solving real problems like the crisis of black male underperformance."[54]* Surely officials at the University of Michigan

---

*Warming to the excoriation of university officials he perceives as having only an "aesthetic" interest in diversifying classrooms, Thomas remarks:

> The Law School seeks only a façade—it is sufficient that the class looks right, even if it does not perform right.
>
> The Law School tantalizes unprepared students with the promise of a University of Michigan degree and all of the opportunities that it offers. These overmatched students take the bait, only to find that they cannot succeed in the cauldron of competition. . . . [T]o cover the tracks of the aestheticists, this cruel force of racial discrimination must continue [in law-review selection and hiring for law firms and judicial clerk-ships] until the beneficiaries are no longer tolerated. While these students may graduate with law degrees, there is no evidence that they have received a qualitatively better legal education (or been better lawyers) then if they had gone to a less "elite" law school for which they were better prepared. And the aestheticists will never address the real problems facing

Law School were concerned about the image of their institution. Would one expect or desire otherwise? But Thomas neglects to offer even a plausible argument for supposing that that is "all" that concerned them. In Michigan and elsewhere it is clear that university officials have sought within the limitations of their institutional mission to fashion policies that might, at least marginally, assist historically oppressed racial minorities. One might well disagree with their calculations and methods. But for Thomas to assert conclusorily that those officials were insincere in their conduct is irresponsible and, indeed, cruel. One might have hoped that a person who had suffered as acutely as Thomas as a result of highly publicized accusations would be more cautious and thoughtful in making accusations of his own. But, alas, all of human history shows that while suffering may sometimes elevate sufferers, usually it does not. A much-maligned target of overwrought charges, Justice Thomas makes overwrought charges himself.

Disappointment is another source of anger at Thomas. "I have often pondered," Judge A. Leon Higginbotham, Jr., remarked, "how is it that Justice Thomas, an African-American, could be so insensitive to the plight of the

---

"underrepresented" minorities, instead continuing their social experiments on other people's children.

Grutter v. Bollinger, 539 U.S. 306, 372 (2003) (Thomas, J., dissenting).

powerless."[55] This disappointment was voiced, too, by the journalist William Raspberry in a column reacting to one of Thomas's most heavily criticized opinions—a dissent in which Thomas expressed his belief that the plaintiff, an injured prison inmate, had not been injured with sufficient severity to invoke properly the Cruel and Unusual Punishment Clause of the federal Constitution.[56] Raspberry wrote:

> To tell you the truth, Clarence, I'm personally embarrassed. . . . I told my friends (your critics) that they should just watch while you surprised your right-wing supporters and confounded our enemies.
>
> But your high-falutin' angels-on-a-pinhead opinion the other day that for prison guards to beat the hell out of a handcuffed and shackled inmate does not "constitute cruel and unusual punishment" (unless the victim winds up in intensive care) confounded only those who tried to cut you some slack.[57]

Another reason that Thomas is deeply resented by many African Americans is that he is seen as an exceedingly selfish person who invokes the imagery of antiblack racism when it suits his personal aims but otherwise ignores or even derides protests against racial oppression.* Regarding this complaint, the key event was the

---

*Some observers also fault Thomas for having publicly castigated his sister because she received welfare assistance. Dramatizing what he saw as the insidious addictiveness of such programs, Thomas is reported to have said of his sister: "She gets mad when the mailman is late with her welfare check. That's how dependent she is. What's

second phase of his Supreme Court confirmation hearings. This phase was precipitated by allegations made by Anita Faye Hill, an aide to Thomas when he was the head of the EEOC.[58] A black Yale Law School alumna, she accused him of having made lewd sexual comments to her and of making unwelcome advances. Thomas categorically denied all of Hill's accusations. Moreover, he lambasted the Judiciary Committee's handling of her allegations, describing its conduct as tantamount to a "high-tech lynching." Facing the Committee in proceedings that transfixed the nation, Thomas condensed his rage into an indictment of his inquisitors:

> This is a circus. It is a national disgrace. And from my standpoint as a black American, as far as I'm concerned, it

---

worse is that now her kids feel entitled to the check, too. They have no motivation for doing better or getting out of that situation." "Thomas's Journey on Path of Self-Help," *New York Times*, July 7, 1991.

Critics have asserted that it was wrong for Thomas to name the person he was putting in such a bad light, that it was even worse to embarrass his own sister, that his indifference to the pain of his blood relative is indicative of the hard-heartedness that makes him indifferent to the pain of his racial kin, that his remarks were calculated to impress potential right-wing political sponsors, and that he had misportrayed his sister by omitting any reference to the difficulties she had encountered. See, e.g., Testimony of Professor Patricia King, *Nomination of Judge Clarence Thomas to Be Associate Justice of the Supreme Court of the United States*. Senate Committee on the Judiciary, vol. 2, p. 269. It should be noted, however, that Thomas did apologize to his sister, that she forgave him, and that she steadfastly supported him during his confirmation ordeal. Timothy M. Phelps and Helen Winternitz, *Capitol Games* (1992), p. 145.

is a high tech lynching for uppity blacks who in any way deign to think for themselves, to have different ideas, and it is a message that unless you kow-tow to an old order, this is what will happen to you, you will be lynched, destroyed, caricatured by a committee of the U.S. Senate, rather than hung from a tree.[59]

Thomas is seldom an impressive wordsmith. But with his career on the line, he voiced the most memorable remarks of the hearings and came up with an arresting image that decisively changed the flow of events. Until he spoke, Hill's charges seemed to have doomed Thomas's candidacy. When Thomas invoked the specter of lynching, however, the tide began to turn.[60] He portrayed himself as a defiant black man who was being unfairly imposed upon by a hypocritical, all-white gang of politicians eager to find some reason, any reason, to prevent an African-American male from attaining a coveted position of authority and honor. Thomas thus expertly played the race card in a fashion that triggered deep-rooted racial loyalties. Imperiled by Hill's allegations and an all-white cadre of senatorial investigators, Thomas sounded an alarm that many blacks responded to by circling the wagons around "the brother in trouble." Polls indicate that his favorability ratings among blacks jumped precipitously after the onset of the inquiry into Hill's charges.[61]

The confrontation between Hill and Thomas was extraordinary. The televised proceedings thrust viewers into a universe of baffling contradictions where, as Professor Kimberlé Crenshaw observes:

political allegiances barely imaginable a moment earlier sprang to life: the administration that won an election through the shameful exploitation of the mythic black rapist took the offensive against stereotypes about black male sexuality; a political party that had been the refuge of white resentment won the support, however momentary, of the majority of African Americans; a black neoconservative individualist . . . was embraced under the wings of racial solidarity; and a black woman, herself a victim of racism, was symbolically transformed into the role of a would-be white woman whose unwarranted finger-pointing whetted the appetites of a racist lynch mob.[62]

The Hill-Thomas confrontation also gave rise to a contest that pitted against each other two narratives of racial betrayal. In one, Thomas was the villain who violated his duties as chair of the Equal Employment Opportunities Commission by sexually harassing a subordinate while stabbing blacks in the back by embracing reactionary racial policies. In the other, Hill was the villain—a black woman who permitted herself to be used by whites to bring low a rapidly rising black man.*

Why is it that in the court of public opinion, Thomas clearly prevailed among blacks as well as whites? Why is

*According to Crenshaw, "Many commentators were less interested in exploring whether the allegations were true than in speculating why Hill would compromise the upward mobility of a black man and embarrass the African-American community. . . . Liberal, centrist, and conservative opinion seemed to accept a view of Hill as disloyal and even treasonous." "Whose Story Is It Anyway? Feminist and Antiracist Appropriations of Anita Hill," in *Race-ing Justice, Engendering Power: Essays on Anita Hill, Clarence Thomas, and the Construction of Social Reality,* Toni Morrison, ed. (1992), p. 420.

it that for most blacks at that time *she* was the sellout (or at least more of a sellout than he)?* Many blacks took the position that, even if Hill's allegations were true, racial solidarity required supporting Thomas. But why? After all, Hill is black, too. Why should African Americans have supported Thomas over her? For many blacks the thinking went like this: the sister should have refrained from telling the white folks news that would imperil the brother's attainment of a powerful position in which he might be able at least occasionally to assist his racial kin. A black woman who is loyal to her race should desist from publicly airing a black man's dirty laundry because white authorities will simply use this information to do what they really want to do anyway—namely, keep blacks in their "place."

Why is it that many African Americans perceived the

---

*Some who embraced Anita Hill during and after the hearings ignored her previous political allegiances. One commentator who did not was the writer Pearl Cleage. Expressing disdain for what she viewed as Hill's unwarranted sanctification, Cleage remarked:

> I still don't understand how Anita Hill became an African American Shero. . . . Does reluctantly agreeing to testify ten years after the crime was committed qualify Sister Anita for a permanent place in the pantheon of black warrior women? . . . Isn't this same Sister Anita the woman who made a choice to work with the enemies of her race and gender? Not as a double agent, gathering inside information and channeling it to her sisters on the front lines, but as a member of the team. As a well-trained collaborator.

Pearl Cleage, *Deals with the Devil and Other Reasons to Riot* (1993), pp. 75–76.

prospect of Thomas's rejection as a potential blow to blacks as a whole? They saw it that way because of a notion of shared fate: whatever happens for good or ill to one black affects "us" all. They were committed to a strategy of communal advancement whereby every "first," every accomplishment, every honor, every promotion by any black was seen as a step upward lifting the entire group. From this perspective, Thomas's fate was a proper rallying point not only for the nominee and his closest circle of intimates; it was a proper rallying point for *all* blacks because, if confirmed, he would constitute a communal asset—an empowered, influential black man (regardless of the content of his ideas or policies).*

An impressive cadre of intellectuals and activists have criticized the sexism embedded in the call for black women aggrieved by black men to abide by a code of silence purportedly for the good of the race as a whole. Professor Kimberlé Crenshaw has been a particularly influential critic of "the patriarchal way that racial solidarity has been defined in the black community."[63]

---

*Professor Manning Marable notes that many blacks believe that "if *individual* African Americans are advanced to the positions of political, cultural or corporate prominence, then the entire black community will benefit. This concept is essentially 'symbolic representation': the conviction that the individual accomplishments of a Bill Cosby, Michael Jordan, Douglas Wilder, or Oprah Winfrey trickle down to empower millions of less fortunate African Americans." Manning Marable, "Clarence Thomas and the Crisis of Black Political Culture," *Race-ing Justice, En-gendering Power: Essays on Anita Hill, Clarence Thomas, and the Construction of Social Reality*, Toni Morrison, ed. (1992), pp. 73–74.

According to Crenshaw, the "vilification of Anita Hill and the embracing of Clarence Thomas [revealed] that a black woman breaking ranks to complain of sexual harassment is seen by many African-Americans as a much greater threat to our group interest than a black man who breaks ranks over race policy."[64]* Crenshaw assails this state of affairs. She upbraids the men who have dissuaded black women from openly sharing their experiences with intraracial mistreatment. But she also upbraids the women whose "own participation in [the] conspiracy of silence has legitimated sexism within our community."[65]

Considerations other than gender and race also played a role in swaying the allegiances of onlookers. Some who sided with Thomas believed that even if what Hill alleged was true, her allegations came too late—over a decade after the claimed harassment. As one observer put it: "[e]ven black people who did not support Clarence Thomas's politics felt that Hill's charges, made public at the eleventh hour, smacked of treachery."[66] Others who sided with Thomas believed that the price of acknowl-

---

*See also Tommie Shelby, *We Who Are Dark: The Philosophical Foundations of Black Solidarity* (2005), p. 227. ("When black women voice, let alone attempt to aggressively deal with, their political concerns . . . this is often wrongly seen as a divisive attempt to embarrass black men or as an imprudent move that threatens to worsen the public image of blacks. Rather than listening to black women and thinking of their concerns as integral to the freedom struggle, many black men have tried to silence them and have remained complicit in the perpetuation of patriarchy often in the name of 'unity.'")

edging the truthfulness of the allegation—namely, the end of Thomas's candidacy—would have been egregiously disproportionate to the seriousness of the infraction in question. This was the point pressed by Professor Orlando Patterson, who hypothesized that the conduct demonized as "sexual harassment" had probably amounted merely to some awkward, misunderstood "down home courting."[67] And then there were observers who sided with Thomas because they found his categorical denial more believable than Hill's hesitant indictment.

At bottom, though, it was feelings of racial loyalty that constituted the main basis for the remarkable uptick in black support that Thomas received during the Anita Hill phase of his confirmation hearings. A protocol of racial loyalty dictated that only in the most dire of emergencies—for example, an immediate need for self-defense—could a "good brother" or "good sister" properly inform upon a fellow black. Because Hill was deemed to have violated this protocol, many blacks initially saw her as the sellout—an impression that provided Thomas with a small but essential edge in his desperate struggle to win confirmation.

Many blacks who came to Thomas's defense now feel that they were "played." They thought that once Thomas "got over" he would act more in accordance with dominant African-American political sensibilities.[68] Instead, Thomas now appears sometimes to delight in affronting African-American public opinion—as when he officiated at the wedding of Rush Limbaugh, the infamous right-wing talk-show host whom many blacks dismiss as an anti-Negro bigot.[69]

Anger at Thomas has been directed toward depriving him of prestige in Black America. This campaign has been largely successful. While his opponents lost the battle to keep him off the Supreme Court, they are winning the battle over his reputation among African Americans. Local anti-Thomas protests regularly make visits by him to law schools and other venues occasions for strife. Consider the controversy that ensued in 2002 when the dean of the University of North Carolina School of Law announced that, with the help of Senator Jesse Helms, he had succeeded in persuading Justice Thomas to visit the school.[70] The visit included an assembly with students (with written questions submitted beforehand) and other sessions of the sort that law schools routinely host to honor leading jurists. The five African Americans on the UNC faculty—the North Carolina Five—declared collectively that they objected to the invitation and would refrain from attending any of his appearances. They conveyed their opposition in an open letter in which they declared that "for many people who hold legitimate expectations for racial equality and social justice, Justice Thomas personifies the cruel irony of the fireboat burning and sinking."[71] The day before Justice Thomas's visit, the Black Law Students Association sponsored an anti-Thomas teach-in at which the five black professors spoke.

Two features of the campaign to ostracize Thomas are especially noteworthy. One is the claim by some detractors that Thomas is professionally substandard and lamentably dependent upon others, particularly his law clerks and Justice Antonin Scalia. There is "no reason even to hope," Carl Rowan mused plaintively, that Justice Thomas "will ever be anything other than a clone of the most conservative Justice, Antonin Scalia."[72] Describing Justice Scalia as the Court's right-wing ideologue, the lawyer-writer Vincent T. Bugliosi referred to Thomas as "his Pavlovian puppet . . . who doesn't even try to create the impression that he's thinking."[73]

Justice Thomas has responded, with understandable anger, to this critique, particularly the accusation that he is Scalia's pawn. "Because I am black," he once remarked, "it is said automatically that Justice Scalia has to do my work for me. That goes with the turf. . . . It is interesting that I rarely see him, so he must have a chip in my brain."[74]

More persuasive than Thomas's cursory rebuttal are the detailed analyses of scholars who, while criticizing certain of the justice's substantive positions, nonetheless conclude that he is an independent jurist whose opinions warrant serious and respectful attention. According to Professor Angela Onwuachi-Willig, "A review of Justice Thomas' jurisprudence reveals that there is no basis for the claim that [he] is a 'Scalia clone' or 'Scalia puppet' and supports the proposition that [he] has been unfairly subjected to the stereotype of black incompetence. . . . Justice Thomas has developed his own jurisprudence as a black conservative, directly and indirectly weaving his own 'raced' ideologies into his opinions."[75]

What most distinguishes Thomas's opinions in the area of race relations is their author's openly expressed concern with what alternative outcomes will mean for blacks.

When Mississippi was sued on the ground that it had failed to disestablish racial segregation in public higher education, Justice Thomas focused on what the Court's ruling would and should entail for the state's historically black colleges and universities (HBCUs).[76] Thomas warmly embraced HBCUs. Acknowledging that they were created by segregation, he stressed their positive achievements and ongoing contributions and insisted that the Court's ruling (in which he concurred) would not require any substantial reformation of their procedures or traditions. Lauding HBCUs as symbols "of the highest attainments of black culture," Thomas cited W. E. B. DuBois. "We must rally to the defense of our schools," DuBois declared. "We must repudiate this unbearable assumption of the right to kill institutions unless they conform to one narrow standard."[77] Thomas concluded by observing that it would be tragically ironic "if the institutions that sustained blacks during segregation were themselves destroyed in an effort to combat its vestiges."[78]

Justice Thomas's opinion in *Missouri v. Jenkins* is another that sounds themes drawn from a distinctively African-American tradition. *Jenkins* involved a challenge to a lower court's order requiring Missouri to finance improvements in the formerly segregated public schools in a predominantly black district with the aim of attracting white students who had previously abandoned or avoided these schools. The Supreme Court reversed the lower court's ruling. According to the Court, the federal judiciary is authorized to remedy state-sponsored segregation—*not* problems in general that have no causal relationship with official segregation. The lower court judge had ordered the school district to adopt programs that would attract whites, create more racial balance, and offset detrimental conditions that, in the judge's view, often plague predominantly black schools. Because the racial imbalance could not be sufficiently linked to state-sanctioned segregation, the lower court overstepped its authority, according to the Supreme Court, in attempting to "cure" or even diminish racial imbalance or its concomitant educational deficiencies.

In a concurring opinion, Thomas joined his white conservative colleagues in insisting that federal judges eschew any temptation to be omnibus social reformers and instead observe strict limits on their authority. Thomas, however, went beyond objections having to do with federalism and judicial competence. He also challenged what he saw as the empirical foundation of the lower court's ruling: the association of a predominantly black presence (i.e., "racial imbalance") with educational deficiency. "It never ceases to amaze me," Thomas wrote with evident pique, "that the courts are so willing to assume that anything that is predominantly black must be inferior."[79]

Thomas insisted upon differentiating state-enforced racial separation and racial separation emanating from personal preferences (that is, blacks choosing to live in mainly black residential enclaves or whites choosing to live in mainly white residential enclaves). In Thomas's view, racially distinctive schools emanating from the former are constitutionally tainted while racially distinctive schools emanating from the latter are unobjectionable.

For Thomas, in other words, the racial demographics of schools are, by themselves, legally irrelevant. What matters is how the racial demographics are created. If they are created by governmental mandate, they stem presumptively from a constitutional violation. But if they are created by private preference, they stem from the legally protected liberty of families to express their values through, among other things, their choice of neighborhoods and schooling. Hence, Thomas finds nothing wrong, per se, with all-white public schools or all-black public schools.

Focusing on the tendency of some observers to see the all-black school as a legal and pedagogical problem, Thomas asserts that "there is no reason to think that black students cannot learn as well when surrounded by members of their own race as when they are in an integrated environment."[80] Moreover, reprising the theme he sounded in *United States v. Fordice* with respect to HBCUs, Thomas in *Jenkins* asserts that schools identifiable as "black schools" should not be dismissed automatically as dysfunctional, for they "can function as the center and symbol of black communities, and provide examples of independent black leadership, success, and achievement."[81] Thomas does not assume that black schools will be educationally sound; he recognizes that many are institutional disasters. He does insist, however, that the condition of being all-black does not, in and of itself, doom an institution to failure.

How a given policy will affect blacks is a consistently expressed consideration in Thomas's opinions. His opposition to affirmative action has to do not so much with alleged unfairness to whites—the central theme of many white conservatives—but instead with his perception that it is bad for blacks. Similarly, regarding school vouchers, Thomas demonstrates a keen interest in what alternative resolutions of the controversy will mean to black American families. In *Zelman v. Simmons-Harris*,[82] the Court upheld the constitutionality of a school-voucher program in Cleveland, Ohio. Plaintiffs charged that the program violated the Establishment Clause of the federal Constitution by funneling public funds for school tuition to public or private schools, including private schools with a religious affiliation. The Court concluded that the program is constitutional in that it is neutral with respect to religion, benefiting a wide spectrum of individuals based on criteria defined by financial need and residential location. Justice Thomas concurred with the Court's holding but added additional reasons in support, one of which is the impact of the voucher program upon "failing urban public schools [that] disproportionately affect minority children most in need of educational opportunity."[83] Lauding voucher programs for addressing "the root of the problem with failing urban public schools" and chiding opponents for raising what he dismisses as "formalistic concerns" about church-state entanglements, Thomas describes vouchers as a method for restoring the lost promise of public education for inner-city blacks:

> While the romanticized ideal of universal public education resonates with the cognoscenti who oppose vouchers, poor

urban families just want the best education for their children, who will certainly need it to function in our high-tech and advanced society. . . . The failure to provide education to poor urban children perpetuates a vicious cycle of poverty, dependence, criminality, and alienation that continues for the remainder of their lives. If society cannot end racial discrimination, at least it can arm minorities with the education to defend themselves from some of discrimination's effects.[84]*

Contrary, then, to what some detractors contend, Justice Thomas articulates viewpoints and theories that are independent of those advanced by his fellow justices. Moreover, he does so in a fashion that is his own, citing a greater number and wider array of black thinkers than any other justice in the history of the Supreme Court. He begins his dissent in *Grutter* with a quotation from Frederick Douglass. He begins his concurrence in *Fordice* with a quotation from W. E. B. DuBois. In his concur-

---

*Another example of Justice Thomas evincing special concern for the effects of a ruling on blacks in particular is *Georgia v. McCollum*, 505 U.S. 42 (1992). In that case, the Supreme Court held that the Equal Protection Clause of the federal Constitution prohibits defense counsel as well as prosecutors from using race as a basis for peremptorily challenging prospective jurors. Justice Thomas joined with the NAACP Legal Defense Fund in decrying rules that would disable black defendants from excluding white prospective jurors for the purpose of opening up space for black jurors. See Randall Kennedy, *Race, Crime, and the Law* (1997), pp. 216–17 (Justice Thomas's "expressed solicitude for black defendants [as opposed to any other type of defendant] seems out of character with his general insistence that the law [including judges] treat all persons the same regardless of race").

rence in *Zelman* he again cites Douglass and pays homage as well to the language and ideas of the person he credits with putting him on the road toward black conservatism—Thomas Sowell. Thomas thus openly taps into black intellectual traditions and honors black intellectual icons. Far from engaging in any effort toward "passing," Thomas in his judicial and extrajudicial statements calls attention to his experiences, identity, and aspirations as a black man keenly concerned with the destiny of black folk. "I am not an Uncle Tom," Thomas insisted in a conference with black journalists, political figures, and entrepreneurs. "I have not forgotten where I came from. I feel a special responsibility to help our people."[85]

Thomas's repeated assertions that he is *not* a racial traitor and that, to the contrary, he feels a "special responsibility to help our people" is noteworthy for at least two reasons. First, they show a likelihood, even probability, that he truly cares about the way blacks in particular view him. He has stated that he feels deeply hurt by the suggestion that he is harming fellow blacks. The best example is his appearance in 1998 at the annual meeting of the National Bar Association (NBA)—a black organization of jurists that originated to serve as an alternative to the American Bar Association (ABA), which long excluded African-American lawyers. The NBA had declined to support Thomas's Supreme Court nomination. Moreover, a large faction within the NBA, led by Judge Higginbotham, attempted to have the organization's invitation to Thomas rescinded. Still, Thomas attended the NBA meeting and sought expressly to win his audience's acceptance, if not approval. Second, Thomas's expressed special concern with African Americans is in tension with his professed attachment to "color blindness" and his assertions that his racial background does not and should not affect his jurisprudence.* An adherent to Thomas's rejection of racial distinctions in the law might well complain about the justice's attentiveness to how this or that law or policy particularly affects black Americans.

The claim, then, that Thomas is an epigone of his conservative colleagues is simply mistaken. He is independent and distinctive. Moreover, as a justice, Thomas is very much a "race man," by which I mean a black person who seeks self-consciously to advance, by his own lights, the interests of African Americans.

This is not an endorsement of Thomas's aims, conclusions, or methods. His jurisprudence is riddled by inconsistencies, evasions, and arbitrariness. He speaks as a near absolutist adherent to the notion of the color-blind Constitution when he condemns affirmative action. But he defers to pragmatic considerations in championing the perpetuation of black public institutions that are vestiges of racial segregation. He complains that it would be a sad

---

*"If we are to be a nation of laws and not of men, judges must be impartial referees. . . . When deciding cases, a judge's race, sex, and religion are all irrelevant. . . . A judge is not a legislator, for whom it is entirely appropriate to consider personal and group interests." Clarence Thomas, "Be Not Afraid," speech to the American Enterprise Institute, Feb. 13, 2001.

irony if the institutions that sustained blacks during segregation were themselves destroyed in an effort to combat its vestiges. Yet he adamantly refuses to see any irony
in prohibiting, on grounds of racial equality, special
efforts to assist the descendants of enslaved or segregated
blacks. He accuses opponents of school voucher programs of being in thrall to "formalistic concerns" about
the Establishment Clause. Yet Thomas is the Court's
principal adherent to the formalistic equation of racial
distinctions intended to impose white supremacy with
racial distinctions intended to undo white supremacy.*
There is no sillier idea than this in all of American law. As
Justice Stevens notes:

> There is no moral or constitutional equivalence between a
> policy [e.g., Jim Crow] that is designed to perpetuate a
> caste system and one that seeks to eradicate racial subordi-
> nation [e.g., affirmative action]. Invidious discrimination is
> an engine of oppression, subjugating a disfavored group to
> enhance or maintain the power of the majority. Remedial
> race-based preferences reflect the opposite impulse: a desire
> to foster equality in society. . . . The consistency that [Jus-
> tice Thomas and the Court] espouses would disregard the
> difference between a "No trespassing" sign and a welcome
> mat.[86†]

* "I believe that there is a moral [and] constitutional equivalence . . .
between laws designed to subjugate a race and those that distribute
benefits on the basis of race in order to foster some current notion of
equality." *Adarand Constructors v. Pena,* 515 U.S., 240. (Thomas, J.,
concurring).
†One need not embrace Thomas's dubious theory of equivalence
in order to oppose affirmative action. One could concede, as one

For all his deficiencies, however, Justice Thomas is a jurist with his own ideas. They are ideas with which I often disagree. But they are *his* ideas. Opponents of the justice do their side no favor by minimizing his capabilities or achievements. He is a force to be reckoned with, and his objectionable positions can be reliably overcome only by careful study and studious rebuttal. The all-too-common practice of simply calling him a "sellout" is a debilitating shortcut that permits opponents to avoid doing the work needed to educate and persuade audiences that are still movable regarding their assessments of the justice.

A second notable feature of the anti-Thomas campaign is that many detractors treat him differently from white jurists on account of his race. When Justices Antonin Scalia and Sandra Day O'Connor visited the University of North Carolina School of Law, the black

---

sensibly should, that invidious discrimination rests on a different moral plane than positive discrimination (i.e., affirmative action) yet still conclude, for various reasons, that the latter is unwise or unlawful. Judge Thomas Gibbs Gee showed this to be so in an opinion voicing his disagreement with the Supreme Court's affirmance of an affirmative-action program. Gee remarked that as a lower court judge he would follow what he perceived to be the Supreme Court's erroneous direction because affirmative action was merely mistaken as opposed to evil. Judge Gee declared that if he thought affirmative action were evil he would have felt honor-bound to resign rather than facilitate a malevolent social policy. Justice Thomas stubbornly refuses to make such distinctions and instead paints with excessively broad strokes, proclaiming all the while that his own personal policy preferences have nothing to do with his rulings as a judge. See *Weber v. Kaiser Aluminum Chemical Corp.*, 611 F.2d 139 (CA5 1980).

professors refrained from publicly protesting their presence even though they had cast votes and made statements that were similar to those that prompted the targeting of Thomas. What accounts for the differential treatment? Some observers attribute it to racism, maintaining that because of Thomas's race, some of his detractors feel emboldened to act toward him in ways they would never consider if he were white. They assert that because of Thomas's blackness he is deprived, to some degree, of the deference routinely conferred upon white justices. They point to statements of the sort made by United States Senator Harry Reid when he objected to the idea of Justice Thomas being appointed chief justice. Thomas, Reid remarked, is an "embarrassment" whose "opinions are poorly written." By contrast, Senator Reid stated that he could support elevating Justice Scalia because he is "one smart guy."* For some observers, the most plausible explanation for Reid's "strikingly different opinions of two justices with similar conservative views is the stereotype of black incompetence."[87] They recall that Thurgood Marshall, too, was disparaged for being less conscientious, less bright, and less effective

---

*See Michael A. Fletcher, "Reid Says He Could Back Scalia for Chief Justice: Comments Anger Liberals and Thomas Supporters," *Washington Post,* Dec. 7, 2004; Zev Chafets, "Slap at Thomas Stinks of Racism," New York *Daily News,* Dec. 8, 2004. For an excellent discussion of this remark in the context of ongoing disputes regarding the racial politics that surround Justice Thomas, see Angela Onwuachi-Willig, "Just Another Brother on the SCT?: What Justice Clarence Thomas Teaches Us About the Influence of Racial Identity," 90 *Iowa Law Review* 931 (2005).

than his (white) colleagues, even though evidence supporting such a charge was absent or equivocal.

Partisans of the theory that racism infects criticism of Justice Thomas maintain that the contagion taints not only attacks launched by whites but attacks launched by blacks as well. Recognizing that blacks, too, have internalized many features of antiblack racism, these partisans maintain that some of Thomas's black opponents go after him with an abandon that they would be inhibited from displaying if their target were a white justice of the Supreme Court. Chief Justice William Hubbs Rehnquist displayed antipathy to antiracist reform as a private attorney and government lawyer. Moreover, as a justice he almost always voted against the positions pressed by those seeking to vindicate the claims of aggrieved racial minority litigants. Yet seldom, if ever, did he face the gauntlets of outraged black protesters that Thomas has had to face regularly.[88] Partisans of the racism theory conclude that while Rehnquist's whiteness provided him with a measure of insulation against vociferous critics, Thomas's blackness offers no such protection but instead elicits an extra measure of emboldened anger.

Claims that racism infects the campaign to ostracize Thomas are difficult to substantiate. Was Senator Reid's different treatment of Scalia and Thomas due to race or did it stem from real differences in the performances of the two justices? (After all, at oral argument at the Supreme Court Scalia is a lively, combative questioner, while Thomas is frequently silent.) But the racism theory is at least plausible. Given the demonstrated capacity of racism to seep into all manner of judgments, it would not be surprising to learn that, in fact, racism had played some role in the extraordinary campaign of disparagement that has targeted Justice Thomas.

While racism is a possible basis for the uniquely negative treatment that Thomas receives, a certain basis is the belief that it is more blameworthy for a black than for a nonblack to embrace positions that are detrimental to the African-American community. This belief was voiced strongly by Judge Higginbotham in a colloquy with Professor Evelyn Wilson, one of the few legal academics who has defended Justice Thomas. Higginbotham wrote an open letter in which he chastised Thomas for his pre–Supreme Court record and urged him to use his new position to chart a different course. Wilson responded by complaining that, on a racial basis, Higginbotham imposed a more restrictive code of conduct on Thomas than on any of his white colleagues.[89] Higginbotham replied by suggesting that it was proper to impose a more demanding standard of expectations on a black than on a nonblack jurist. The Dred Scott decision was evil and tragic, Higginbotham asserted. "But think of what an even greater tragedy it would have been if, in 1857, a Black had been on the Supreme Court and had joined in the majority's opinion."[90]

Absent from Judge Higginbotham's analysis, unfortunately, is any explanation for his belief. Perhaps embedded in his thinking is a notion that a black person knows (or should know) better than a nonblack about the detrimental consequences wrought by racist policies. Maybe the theory is that to persist in embracing such policies despite superior knowledge makes the black person more morally culpable than his nonblack peer, who has the excuse of ignorance. We should resist, however, the tendency to infer that a person is knowledgeable about a given subject just because he or she is of some given social status—a black, a white, a man, or a woman. Some commentators believe that people of color, because of their collective experience as victims of racial oppression, have enhanced knowledge and insight about race relations or at least the colored side of race relations.[91] There are, however, a sufficient number of examples that run counter to that hypothesis—Clarence Thomas himself is a striking instance—to warrant considerable caution in making such generalizations. Rather than assuming greater knowledge on account of race and then suffering deeper disappointment when that expectation is unfulfilled, it would be better to refrain from making strong assumptions based on racial status and instead to investigate directly a person's knowledge and sensibilities.[92]

Yet another source of the racially distinctive anger directed at Thomas derives from the perception that, because of his race, he is especially well positioned to do damage to blacks. Again consider the North Carolina Five. They acknowledge that they responded differently to Justice Thomas than to his conservative white colleagues. They maintain, however, that there is a good reason for their racially disparate response: Thomas's blackness gives him an edge in ideological combat over racial issues—an edge in terms of perceived authenticity that he and his right-wing allies are quick to exploit.[93] Inasmuch as Thomas and his allies deploy his blackness strategically, opponents see nothing wrong with calling attention to this fact and taking it into account in their own efforts to counteract the Thomas camp. The North Carolina Five puts it this way:

> While the political right does not need Justice Thomas to push its agenda . . . it does need him to put a black face on that agenda. . . . For all its talk of colorblindness, the political right realizes that Justice Thomas will not be an effective icon of racial conservatism until African Americans ourselves accept and embrace him.[94]*

The black professors treated Thomas differently from Scalia, then, because they saw the former as a more dangerous foe. They perceived Thomas's blackness as offering him a distinctive weapon. It armed him with a calling card to Afro-America that no white jurist possessed. African Americans' initial tendency to see Thomas as a "brother," to enjoy vicariously his personal success (despite his ideological leanings), and to give him the benefit of the doubt on the strength of a putative racial kinship are what the North Carolina Five feared, what

*Explaining why it decided to oppose Thomas's confirmation for a seat on the Supreme Court, the Board of Directors of the NAACP wrote: "Precisely because he is an African American, Thomas may be even more effective than a white conservative . . . in legitimizing [attacks upon] the civil rights principles critical to African Americans." Quoted in Ken Foskett, *Judging Thomas: The Life and Times of Clarence Thomas* (2004), p. 222.

sets Thomas apart from his white colleagues on the right, and what prompts some detractors to ostracize him with special rigor. For them, to expose the strategic deployment of Thomas's blackness by the justice and his allies is not racism but realism in the service of progressive racial politics.

Large numbers of Americans see Clarence Thomas as a sellout. Is he? That depends on the governing definition of the term. If a sellout is a citizen of Black America who is merely wrong regarding important matters of racial politics then Thomas can rightly be labeled a sellout. But those who prosecute Thomas for racial betrayal assert that he is guilty of more than being wrong. They imply or assert that he deliberately harms Black America, or knows that he does so without a justification or excuse, or pursues a dangerous course of action without heed of consequences. Hence Professor Crenshaw decries Thomas's "unbounded willingness to stymie the advancement of other African Americans."[95] Similarly, Judge Higginbotham asserts that Thomas "willfully crippled African-American interests."[96] It is one thing to charge someone with hurting the cause of African Americans. It is another to charge someone with *knowingly* or *willfully* hurting that cause. It is the knowingness or the willfulness that makes "selling out" so reprehensible. Yet Crenshaw and Higginbotham forgo adducing evidence of any purposeful or knowing misconduct on Thomas's part. Nor do they demonstrate that there has been indifference or recklessness on Thomas's part—what in legal lingo is called gross negligence. Higginbotham in particu-

lar proceeds as if malevolence (or psychopathology)* is
the only believable explanation behind Thomas's race-
relations jurisprudence. But what about the rationales
that Thomas offers to justify his conclusions? Are they
utterly groundless? And what about the appreciable
number of African Americans who agree with Thomas?
Is anyone who rejects affirmative action as a matter of
policy or constitutional law a closeted racist or, in the
case of a black, a sellout?

The arguments Thomas posits to justify his conclusions are sufficiently weighty to defeat the naked infer-
ence that they are simply makeweights cobbled together
to camouflage beliefs too shameful to be candidly
announced. One need not accept at face value the reasons a judge (or anyone else) offers for his or her conclusions. They may be pretexts covering the actual reasons
behind a given ruling—reasons that may be hidden even
from the judge himself. If one attributes to a judge an
unarticulated belief or goal, however, it is essential to
explain why the proffered explanation for a decision—

---

*Along with remarking that Thomas's views are "just as extreme and
harmful" as the views expressed in the notorious Supreme Court rulings in *Dred Scott v. Sandford* (making blacks ineligible for federal
citizenship) and *Plessy v. Ferguson* (upholding the constitutionality of
state-compelled racial segregation), Judge Higginbotham contended
that "there must be some mystical force . . . that compels Justice
Thomas to some of his persistently absurd and hostile anti-minority
decisions, and it may very well be attributable to factors of a racial
self-hatred that not even he fully comprehends." Higginbotham,
"Justice Clarence Thomas in Retrospect," 45 *Hastings Law Journal*
1405 (1993), pp. 1424, 1429.

say, the aim to stymie blacks—is a more realistic explanation for the decision than the one that the judge proffers—in this case, the belief that affirmative action itself stymies blacks. Regarding Justice Thomas, this has not been done.

It might be objected that I am taking charges of "selling out" all too seriously, that "sellout" is merely a vague figure of speech commonly understood as rhetorical hyperbole. I contend, though, that what might have been understood initially as strategic exaggeration has now become widely accepted as an accurate assessment of Justice Thomas's jurisprudence—an assessment that obscures weaknesses as well as strengths in Thomas's arguments. What I am urging is not condonation of his views but merely an informed understanding of them that provides a predicate for carefully calibrated criticism. Words should matter. To denounce someone as a sellout should matter. The fact that some detractors of Justice Thomas have publicly voiced hopes for his early demise is reason enough to reconsider the justice of the vilification that follows him.

It might also be objected that I have made it too difficult to convict on charges of racial betrayal, reducing the pool of race traitors to an illusory null set. After all, if Clarence Thomas is not a sellout, then who is?

I do impose requirements that place considerable burdens on those seeking convictions for racial betrayal in the court of public opinion. That is proper, however, given the seriousness of the charge in question. If Thomas's detractors want to avoid my burdensome requirements, all they need do is lower the level of their disparagement. Instead of calling Thomas a "sellout," detractors could accuse him of being ignorant, stupid, or foolish—bad attributes, to be sure, but ones lacking the peculiarly disgracing culpability associated with traitorousness.

Under my criteria, who could properly be deemed a sellout? Here are some examples: an African-American member of a black uplift organization who reveals its secrets to antiblack adversaries out of malevolence or merely for purposes of self-promotion; an African American who, believing that a given position is adverse to the interest of blacks, advances that position anyway for patently unjustifiable reasons; a black person who, though believing he is helping blacks, supports a seriously harmful policy for which there exists not even a plausible excusing argument.

If we look to the recent history of homosexuals, another group facing widespread invidious discrimination, we encounter a number of prominent closeted gays who have actively supported expressly antigay politicians, organizations, or policies. Terry Dolan (who died of AIDS) was a founder and director of the National Conservative Political Action Committee (NCPAC) when it openly appealed to antigay prejudice to mobilize right-wing voters.[97] Robert Bauman (whose career was shattered when he was arrested for soliciting sex with a male minor) was a conservative Republican member of the House of Representatives who vocally condemned homosexuality.[98] Arthur J. Finkelstein (who married his male companion in Massachusetts, where they reside as the adoptive parents of two children) worked on behalf of the NCPAC and several militantly antigay politicians, including, most notably, Senator Jesse Helms, a leading homophobe during his tenure in Congress.[99]

There are few, if any, influential African Americans who champion politicians, organizations, or policies that are openly antiblack.* This is not a matter of some peculiarly African-American virtue. It has to do with the comparative status of frank Negrophobia versus frank homophobia. While there is not much of a political market for the former, there is an ample political market for the latter. Regardless of a person's sexual orientation, he often stands to gain by openly evincing support for invidious discrimination against gays and lesbians. Hence the broad support of ambitious politicians for legal distinctions that burden gays and lesbians in the armed services and family life. By contrast, regardless of a person's race, he rarely stands to gain by openly evincing support for

---

*The key modifier here is "influential," because there are blacks who knowingly support antiblack racists. An intriguing example is James Meredith, who sparked a national crisis in 1962 when he became the first self-identified black to matriculate at the University of Mississippi. See *Meredith v. Fair*, 298 F.2d. 696 (CA 5 1962).; William Doyle, *An American Insurrection: The Battle of Oxford, Mississippi, 1962* (2001). Meredith subsequently worked for Senator Jesse Helms and endorsed the infamous former Ku Klux Klansman David Duke when he ran for governor of Louisiana in 1991. See Kimberly Hayes Taylor, "King-Sized Impact," *Star Tribune*, Jan. 14, 2000. Duke was not a politician for whom racism was a marginal feature of his persona; it was a central element of his appeal. A historic figure of the 1960s, Meredith subsequently has been more of an oddity than an influence.

invidious racial discriminations against blacks. There is a
political and social payoff for selling out in the context
of conflict regarding sexual orientation that is simply
unavailable in the context of conflict over race.

It might be argued that black sellouts are engaged in
racial betrayal but in a guise that has adapted to changing conditions. Since formal adherence to white supremacy is so stigmatized that only marginal figures openly
advance that sort of racial politics, enemies of African-
American uplift have adopted more nuanced—that is to
say, more deceptive—approaches. They are willing to
denounce egregious acts of obviously racist misconduct.
But they are unwilling to discern racism in any action
that contains the least bit of complexity. They are willing
to acknowledge that blacks have been subjected to racial
subordination historically. But they are unwilling to
demand or even tolerate efforts to repair injuries caused
by such oppression. They profess to be interested in elevating black communities but are not sincerely concerned with doing so. The twenty-first-century version
of the savvy black sellout does not fight for ideological
territory that has been irretrievably lost—for example,
"freedom" to engage in invidious racial discrimination.
Instead, sponsored by white reactionaries, he fights for
ideological territory that remains sharply contested—for
example, the legitimacy of using racial criteria to create
or maintain at least a modicum of racial diversity in
schooling, employment, and governance.

I do not reject the possibility that investigation will
unearth black figures who fit this model of the savvy

black sellout. I simply insist that assessments be scrupulous in the handling of evidence, attentive to the complexity of motives, attuned to the costs of surveillance, and aware that sensible people can, in good faith, seek common aims by different, even fiercely conflicting means. Investigations undertaken with that ethos will give rise to few indictments for racial betrayal. Diminishing the incidence of such claims would be good for Black America.

Five

PASSING AS SELLING OUT

"Nothing is more fundamental to the current iden-tity debates . . . than the issue of choice versus ascription."

David A. Hollinger,
"Identity in the United States" (2004)

The paradigmatic racial passer is the "White Negro,"*
a person who holds himself out as "white," though,
according to ascendant rules of racial designation, the
person is really "black."[1] I am not talking about a person who is mistaken about his background; perhaps
he has been deceptively told that his parents were white.†
Nor am I talking about a person whose appearance
leads observers to think of him as white in the absence of
any purposeful conduct on his part that reinforces this

---

*Norman Mailer wrote a famous essay, "The White Negro: Superfi-
cial Reflection on the Hipster," first published in *Dissent* in 1956.
Notwithstanding its title, it has little to do with the subject under discussion here.
†See the extraordinary memoir by Gregory Howard Williams, *Life on
the Color Line: The True Story of a White Boy Who Discovered He
Was Black* (1995).

(mis)perception.* The White Negro to whom I refer is an individual who presents himself as "white" knowing that he would be seen as "black" if the racial facts of his ancestry were known to observers. This person self-consciously hides or misrepresents such facts in order to be known as white.

White Negroes have often been charged with betraying African Americans by abandonment or complicity in maintaining an illicit racial hierarchy. Are such charges valid? Is it right to "out" passers ensconced in racial closets? Ought people be free to reinvent themselves racially without social disapproval?

Let's begin by considering the circumstances in which "blacks" have held themselves out as "whites." Passing can be divided into two categories. One is temporary passing, in which the passer goes over to the white side with the intention of rejoining the African-American community at some point. The other is permanent passing, in which the passer intends to leave the African-American community forever. Temporary passing is a venture in pretense: the person in question pretends to be white for a discrete period of time. Permanent passing is

---

*The line between innocent silence and fraudulent silence can be thin. Consider the reflections of the narrator in James Weldon Johnson's *The Autobiography of an Ex-Coloured Man* (1927, 1989): "I finally made up my mind that I would neither disclaim the black race nor claim the white race; but that I would change my name, raise a moustache, and let the world take me for what it would; that it was not necessary for me to go about with a label of inferiority pasted across my forehead." Id., p. 190.

a venture in conversion: the person in question actually attempts to become white.

In the antebellum period, enslaved blacks who appeared to be white often fled bondage by seeking to pass. An extraordinary instance occurred in 1848, when Ellen Craft—the daughter of a master and his slave mistress—escaped from bondage by train, boat, and carriage on a four-day journey from Macon, Georgia, to Philadelphia, Pennsylvania. Ellen pretended to be white. Her enslaved husband was part of her disguise; he pretended to be her servant. Ellen, moreover, traveled not as a woman but as a man; to obtain freedom for herself and her husband, she temporarily traversed gender as well as racial lines.* As soon as the Crafts reached territory in which they were no longer menaced by immediate re-enslavement, however, she tore off her masks and reclaimed her identity as a Negro.†

---

*The Crafts' planning was extraordinary. Since Ellen could not write, they placed her right arm in a sling to avoid any requests that she sign documents certifying her ownership of her slave. To dissuade strangers from seeking to strike up a conversation with Ellen Craft, William Craft put a poultice on his wife's face. See William Craft, *Running a Thousand Miles for Freedom: The Escape of William and Ellen Craft from Slavery* (1860). See also R. J. M. Blackett, "The Odyssey of William and Ellen Craft" in the Louisiana University Press 1999 edition of *Running a Thousand Miles for Freedom*; Ellen M. Weinauer, "A Most Respectable Looking Gentleman": Passing, Possession, and Transgression in *Running a Thousand Miles for Freedom*," in *Passing and the Fictions of Identity*, Elaine K. Ginsberg, ed. (1996).

†When the Crafts' escape was publicized, they became vulnerable to recapture. Indeed, slave catchers from Georgia attempted to arrest

Blacks have engaged in temporary passing in many other, less dire settings. To advance occupational ambitions, some have passed as white during the workday while presenting themselves as African American outside the workplace.* Other blacks have passed as white in order to shop, sleep, or eat meals at racially exclusive establishments. In their classic *Black Metropolis: A Study of Negro Life in a Northern City,* St. Clair Drake and Horace R. Cayton reported that some light-skinned Negroes in Chicago whom they interviewed in the 1940s spoke of going to white establishments "just to see what they are like and to get a thrill."[2]

Although temporary passing has usually represented efforts to flee racial subordination, the civil rights activist Walter White passed for white in order to expose the worst excesses of Jim Crow violence.[3] Fair-skinned, blue-eyed, and blond-haired, White was the son of light-complexioned Negroes who were listed as "white" in the census of 1900.[4] His mother worked at home while his

---

them in Boston in 1850. They fled to England and returned only after the outbreak of the Civil War. See R. J. M. Blackett, "The Odyssey of William and Ellen Craft."

*Chronicling this phenomenon in "White by Day . . . Negro by Night," a 1952 article in *Ebony* magazine relates the following story:

One girl who passed to get work as a clerk in a Chicago loop department store thought she had lost her job when an old-time, well-meaning friend of her mother came in and said in happy surprise, "Well, Baby, it sure is good to see this store is finally hiring colored girls." Fortunately she was overheard only by one other clerk, who was a liberal and a good friend of the girl who was passing, and her secret did not get out.

father was a mail carrier. Because of their coloring, the Whites frequently found themselves in the middle of racial misunderstandings. When Walter White's mother and sisters boarded segregated streetcars, for example, white men who believed the women to be white often jeered them when they sat in the Negro section. A much more serious racial misunderstanding occurred in 1931, when Walter White's father was struck by an automobile driven by a white physician who practiced at Atlanta's Grady Hospital. At that time, the hospital was divided into two sections. The white section was clean and renovated, the black section dirty and dilapidated. The physician took White's father to the white section of the hospital. Before long, though, a visit by a son-in-law apprised the hospital staff of their "error." Recounting the episode in his autobiography, Walter White wrote that his father "was snatched from the examination table lest he contaminate the 'white' air, and taken hurriedly across the street in a driving downpour . . . to the 'Negro' ward," where he died sixteen days later.[5]

White recalls deciding at an early age to stay on the colored side of the race line. He maintained that the formative event that molded his sense of communal attachment was the Atlanta riot of 1906. Goaded by false stories of Negro men raping white women, a white mob terrorized blacks in Georgia's capital. Caught in town amid marauding whites, young Walter and his father escaped serious injury only because of their light complexions. That camouflage, however, did not prevent a white mob from advancing on the Whites' home. His father determined that he and his son would defend the family homestead with firearms if necessary. White recalls that his father said to him "[i]n a voice as quiet as though he were asking me to pass him sugar at the breakfast table . . . 'Son, don't shoot until the first man puts his foot on the lawn and then—don't you miss." "In that instant," White relates, "there opened up within me a great awareness; I knew who I was. I was a Negro, a human being with an invisible pigmentation which marked me as a person to be hunted, hanged, abused, discriminated against, kept in poverty and ignorance, in order that those whose skin was white would have readily at hand a proof of their superiority," so that "[n]o matter how low a white man fell, he could always hold fast to the smug conviction that he was superior to two-thirds of the world's population."[6]

According to White, the mob never attacked his family's house; it quickly retreated when fired upon by White's black neighbors.*

Years later, White devoted much of his attention to defending African Americans against racially motivated violence. His principal means of struggle was exposure; on behalf of the NAACP, he gathered facts about lynchings and other atrocities and carefully publicized them in an effort to arouse American public opinion. The daring

---

*Professor Kenneth Robert Janken calls into question the accuracy of White's account. He suggests that White fabricated the story of his defense of the home partly to quiet black critics who questioned his race loyalty. *White: The Biography of Walter White, Mr. NAACP* (2003), p. 18.

way in which he pursued this task brought him close to danger. In 1919, he traveled to Phillips County, Arkansas, to investigate the deaths of some two hundred and fifty blacks killed in an effort to discourage collective organization by African-American cotton farmers. When whites in Phillips County became aware of White's purpose, he was forced to escape hurriedly. "You're leaving mister, just when the fun is going to start," White recalls being told by the conductor of the train on which he made his getaway. "A damned yellow nigger is down here passing for white and the boys are going to get him." "No matter what the distance," White later observed, "I shall never take as long a train ride as that one seemed to be."[7]*

The phenomenon of permanent passing also has a long history. Several of the children that Thomas Jefferson sired by his slave Sally Hemings eventually passed for white. Beverly and Harriet Hemings transformed themselves into whites in the early 1820s, shedding their

---

*Walter White wrote a novel, *Flight* (1926), in which passing is a major theme. He remained deeply interested in the phenomenon throughout his life. In 1949, he suggested that dermatological experiments had opened the way for turning into reality the "dream" of making black skin white. That he viewed the prospect of large-scale passing by blacks in a positive light is especially noteworthy given that he himself declined to pass. White championed exploring ways to change skin color because, in his view, "[t]he whole progress of civilization has been a constant enlargement of human freedom—in other words, of human *choice*," and a workable means of race-changing could provide "a new avenue for enlarging the range of human free choice." See "Can Science Conquer the Race Line," *Look*, Aug. 30, 1949.

African-American racial identities at the same time that they fled slavery at Monticello. The experience of their siblings was more complicated. Eston Hemings was emancipated in 1827 by Thomas Jefferson's will, along with his older brother Madison Hemings. The brothers remained in Virginia with their mother until her death, in 1835, at which point they moved to southern Ohio. By then both had started families of their own with mixed-race women who, like them, were descendants of relationships between masters and slaves. The status, color, and racial background of the Hemings brothers' mates were unlikely to have been accidental. As the historians Lucia Stanton and Dianne Swann-Wright observe, both men probably sought marriages that would ensure that their children would inherit, in addition to freedom, "a passport to upper-class status within the black community and the probable option to enter the white race."[8]

In Ohio, Madison Hemings distinguished himself as a carpenter, while Eston Hemings made a name for himself as a professional musician. Madison was content to stay within the small black community of the rural area in which they lived, but Eston seems to have wanted to cross the race line. There was, however, a problem. "Notwithstanding all his accomplishments," one journalist remarked, there existed "an impassable gulf" between Eston Hemings and whites, "even the lowest of them."[9] As another journalist later commented, "a nigger was a nigger in those days and that settled it."[10] The Hemings brothers were white under Virginia law and maybe white under Ohio law as well.[11] As a matter of social practice, however, whites deemed anyone with a "visible admixture" of colored blood to be a Negro. Eston Hemings was described as being only "very slightly colored."[12] But for most whites in that locale even a mere slight coloration was sufficient to stigmatize him.

While Madison Hemings stayed in Ohio and became a much respected member of his local black community, Eston Hemings left. Frustrated by racial exclusion from the jury, the witness stand, the voting booth, and public schools, he moved his family to Madison, Wisconsin, where he adopted a new name and racial identity.* He became Eston H. Jefferson, a white man.

The children of Madison and Eston Hemings identified themselves as whites. Madison's son, William Beverly Hemings, served in an all-white regiment in the Civil War. Another son, James Madison Hemings, disappeared and is thought by some in the family to have silently become white. Neither of these sons married, perhaps fearing that doing so would entail revealing their closeted racial background.† Eston Hemings's daughter, Anna, lived as a white woman and married a white man. Both of her brothers served as officers in white regiments in

---

*In 1845, a Cleveland newspaper wrote, perhaps with Eston Hemings in mind, that, "notwithstanding all the services and sacrifices of Jefferson in the establishment of the freedom of this country, his own son, now living in Ohio, is not allowed a vote, or an oath in a court of justice!" Quoted in Stanton and Swann-Wright, "Bonds of Memory," p. 165.

†On the other hand, perhaps they were gay or simply disliked the bonds of marriage.

the Union Army. One of them, Beverly F. Jefferson, married a white woman and lived a comfortable life as the owner of a prosperous hotel. The other, John Wayles Jefferson, remained single and became a wealthy cotton broker.

Some members of the Hemings family identified themselves as African Americans. During World War II, one of Madison Hemings's descendants was assigned to a white military unit but refused to join it, demanding instead that he be assigned to a black unit. In the 1970s, when Madison Hemings's great-great-great-grandson was but a youngster he called himself black even when a white neighborhood tough pummeled him repeatedly, reportedly screaming, "You're white, I know you're white."[13] To a very large extent, though, members of the Hemings family chose to become white.

The children of Michael Morris Healy—a white, Irish-born Georgia planter—and Eliza Clark, one of his slaves, offer another remarkable example of permanent passing.[14] Prevented by state law from freeing his slaves, Michael Healy sent his children to the North, where they could be educated and also be free of bondage in the event of their father's demise. Several of these children had notable careers. James Augustine Healy (1830–1900) was a member of the first graduating class of the College of the Holy Cross in Worcester, Massachusetts. He pursued clerical studies in Canada and France, became a priest in Boston, and served for twenty-five years as the Catholic bishop of Portland, Maine. Alexander Sherwood Healy (1836–1875) studied music and canon law in Rome and served as rector of the Catholic cathedral in Boston. Michael Augustine Healy (1839–1904) became a captain in the Revenue Cutter Service, the precursor to the Coast Guard, and commanded an ice ship off the coast of Alaska. Patrick Francis Healy (1834–1910) graduated from Holy Cross, joined the Society of Jesus, studied at several of Europe's most elite universities, and eventually became the president of Georgetown University.

Helped by luck and talent, the Healys were also assisted in pursuing their ambitions by wealth, the absence of characteristic Negroid features (except for Alexander Sherwood Healy), and an emotional stance toward their ambiguous racial status that allowed them, with apparent ease, to separate themselves from African Americans. Slavery provided the capital investment that generated the income that fueled the Healys' upward mobility. After their father died, his slaves were hired out and then sold for a substantial sum that provided the Healy children with trust funds.*

For the most part, the Healy children were perceived to be "white." As mentioned above, Alexander Sherwood Healy was darker than his siblings. According to one observer, his African blood "shews [*sic*] distinctly in

---

*When a slave woman named Margaret sued for her freedom in 1856, agents for the Healy estate contested her claim and prevailed in court, whereupon she was immediately sold, together with three of her children, each of them to a different purchaser. James M. O'Toole, *Passing: Race, Religion, and the Healy Family, 1820–1920* (2002), pp. 47–48.

his exterior."[15] Apparently, though, the Catholic bureaucracy averted its eyes from this "taint." So, too, did it avert its eyes from the fact that the parents of the Healy children had never properly married. This might have posed an insuperable barrier to those of the Healys who sought advancement within Catholicism, since, under canon law, special dispensation was required to ordain a candidate for the priesthood who was illegitimate. In the case of the Healys, though, the Catholic hierarchy simply looked the other way.

The Healys made that easy to do. They kept as quiet as possible the facts of their origins, distanced themselves from blacks, and declined to take any notable actions that would advance African Americans. When a black seminarian from Maryland wrote to James Healy requesting an assignment for parish work in the Portland diocese, Healy rebuffed the request, explaining that there were so few black Catholics in Maine "that it would be idle for me to think of adopting you as a subject."[16] The Healys' noninvolvement in racial matters, however, reflected more than a mere tactical decision. It reflected their belief that they were white and thus superior to blacks. When James Healy attended Holy Cross he noted in his diary without objection the comments of classmates regarding "the niggers." On graduation night he attended, without any apparent sense of irony, a blackface minstrelsy show. He dismissed as "a fool" William Lloyd Garrison and delighted that at a rally local abolitionists managed to raise only $1.47 for the purchase of a slave whom they intended to free. A Unionist in the Civil War, Healy opposed the racial egalitarianism of Radical Republicans, concerned that they would wrongly subordinate the restoration of sectional harmony to "the protection, the equalization & the super-elevation of the negro."[17] He and his siblings were conservative, religiously devout individualists who thought of themselves as white even if, with a full understanding of their lineage, most Americans would have classified them otherwise. An ironic aspect of the Healys' saga is that they have been made into blacks posthumously by those who claim them as African-American pioneers. In *The Negro Almanac* Healy is described proudly as "the first Negro Catholic Bishop in the United States," a distinction that he would have vehemently disavowed.[18]

Another person who has been claimed as a black pioneer though she passed for white during much of her lifetime is Anita Hemmings, whom Vassar College touts as its first black graduate. Born in Boston, Hemmings matriculated at Vassar in 1893. Soon before graduation, a roommate, suspecting that something might be awry, asked her father to investigate the Hemmings family. In the course of doing so he learned of their Negritude and revealed Anita Hemmings's secret. Although students and teachers felt betrayed by what they perceived as Anita's deceit, college officials permitted her to graduate. Her attempt at passing, however, did become fodder for newspapers. According to a story in the *World:*

> Society and educational circles . . . are profoundly shocked
> by the announcement . . . that one of the graduating class

of Vassar College this year was a Negro girl, who conceal-
ing her race, entered the college, took the four year's
course, and finally confessed the truth to a professor. . . .
She has been known as one of the most beautiful young
women who ever attended the great institution of learning,
and even now women who receive her in their homes as
their equal do not deny her beauty. . . . [H]er manners were
those of a person of gentle birth, and her intelligence and
ability were recognized alike by her classmates and professors.[19]*

Passing has generated a wide range of responses, some
of the most incisive of which are found in novels. The
treatment of passing that best illuminates Black American fears of abandonment is George S. Schuyler's *Black
No More: Being an Account of the Strange and Wonderful Workings of Science in the Land of the Free, A.D.
1933–1940*.[20] Published in 1931, *Black No More* is the
story of what occurs following the discovery of a medical
process that can conveniently turn black people white. In
Schuyler's mordant narrative blacks quickly and fervently seize the opportunity to become white. In their
frenzied exodus from blackness, Schuyler's Negro characters desert their churches, colleges, sororities, fraternities, and political organizations. "In straining every nerve
to get the Black-No-More treatment," Schuyler writes,

---

*Hemmings's choice of a marital partner further enmeshed her in
passing. She married a White Negro physician, Andrew Love, who
himself passed in order to build a prosperous medical practice that
catered to the rich on Madison Avenue in New York City. Their
daughter, Ellen Love, a 1927 graduate of Vassar, also passed.

"the colored folk forgot all loyalties, affiliations and responsibilities."[21]

Schuyler deepens the lacerating sharpness of his satire by envisioning a racial migration that includes not only the Negro rank and file but also the Negro leadership. Initially black leaders urge their constituents to forgo the Black-No-More medical treatment. Forming the Committee for the Preservation of Negro Racial Integrity, they call upon their followers to show group solidarity and racial pride. When that fails they appeal to the United States Attorney General to take legal action. When that also fails, they join the crowds of blacks who seek "chromatic emancipation."[22]

While Schuyler's satirical portrayal of passers is leavened by humor, the more typical response has been straightforward condemnation. Aggrieved slave owners viewed passing runaways as treacherous thieves who were absconding with valuable property—themselves! White supremacists condemned passing as an insidious danger that threatened the very foundations of the nation. White Negroes, it was feared, would pollute white bloodlines by marrying unsuspecting Caucasians.

Black opponents of white supremacy have also objected to passing. They have done so on a variety of grounds, including the argument that, despite the benefits of racial privilege, passers sacrifice more than they gain. They sacrifice familial ties, friendships, communal affiliations, and the oft-overlooked opportunities afforded by African-American life. The literature on passing is filled with heartrending scenes featuring White

Negroes who fall to pieces because of anxiety over being found out,* White Negroes who face recrimination from white friends and lovers, who, upon learning the racial truth of the case, feel betrayed, and White Negroes, who, for fear of being unmasked, ignore, reject, or deceive even their closest relatives. In Jessie Redmon Fauset's novel *Comedy, American Style* (1933), a mother introduces her son as her butler. In Langston Hughes's short story "Passing," a son walks past his mother without acknowledging her.[†] In Sutton Griggs's *The Hindered Hand* (1895) and Walter White's *Flight* (1926), parents exile children whose dark skin threatens to expose the adults' racial masquerade. In Fannie Hurst's *Imitation of Life* (1933), a passing Negro woman gets herself sterilized to avoid the possibility that a dark-skinned baby would reveal her hidden Negritude. The intended lesson

---

*Bewailing the anxiety with which he contends, a White Negro passer in Frank J. Webb's *The Garies and Their Friends* (1857; reprint 1957) remarks: "[T]his secret in my bosom . . . gnaws, gnaws, gnaws . . . No escaped galley-slave . . . lived in more constant fear of detection; and yet I must nourish this torment secret, and keep it growing in my breast until it has crowded out every honorable and manly feeling." Id., 235.

[†]Dear Ma,

I felt like a dog, passing you downtown last night and not speaking to you. You were great, though. Didn't give a sign that you even knew me, let alone I was your son. If I hadn't had the girl with me, Ma, we might have talked. . . . Isn't she sweet to look at, all blond and blue-eyed. We're making plans [to get married]. . . . I will take a box at the Post Office for your mail. . . . I'm glad there's nothing to stop letters from

of many of these tales is that only someone with lamentably distorted values would subordinate his or her association with relatives and friends to an ambition of upward mobility realizable solely through racial deception. Some authors have expressed this message through the remorseful voice of the passer who rues the choice he or she made. In *Waiting for the Verdict* (1868), Rebecca Harding Davis has a character exclaim that because of his passing he feels that he has "turned his back on blacks" and is "a cheat and a coward." In *Of One Blood* (1902), Pauline Hopkins has a passer confess that he has "played the coward's part in hiding his origins." In *The Autobiography of an Ex-Coloured Man,* James Weldon Johnson has his protagonist assert glumly that by passing he had become a "coward" and "deserter."

The most sustained critique of passing as abandonment is found in *Iola Leroy, or, Shadows Uplifted,* a novel published in 1892 by the distinguished black activist and writer Frances Ellen Watkins Harper (1825–1911). *Iola Leroy* chronicles the life of a light-skinned Negro woman who refuses to pass. The daughter of a master and a slave whom he freed and married, Iola Leroy looks like a white woman, as did her mother.

---

crossing the color line. Even if we can't meet often, we can write, can't we, Ma?

With love from your son,

Jack

Langston Hughes, *The Ways of White Folks* (1933; reprint 1990), pp. 51–55.

Indeed, throughout her childhood, Iola believed herself to be white because her parents shielded her from knowledge about her black ancestry. During the Civil War, Dr. Gresham, a white physician in the Union Army, proposes to her. He tells Iola that he knows of her racial background but wants to marry her anyway. "Love, like faith," he observes, "laughs at impossibilities. I can conceive of no barrier too high for my love to surmount."[23]

Attracted to Dr. Gresham, Iola rejects his offer nonetheless because of her determination "to cast [her] lot with the freed people as a helper, teacher, and friend."[24] In her view, Gresham's proposal creates a stark choice. She could marry him, which would ultimately entail, she believes, becoming white. Or she could reject him, stand with her people, and stay black. She chooses the latter.

To make sure that readers get the message that Iola Leroy made the correct choice, Harper reiterates the necessity of choosing racial sides. Years after Iola refuses Gresham the first time, Harper creates a scene in which her heroine refuses him again:

> I don't think that I could best serve my race by forsaking them and marrying you. . . . I must serve the race which needs me most.[25]

Harper also creates scenes in which other pale-skinned Negroes heroically eschew passing. At the outset of the Civil War, Iola's brother, Harry Leroy, tells the headmaster at his New England preparatory school that he would like to volunteer for service in the Union Army. When the headmaster points out that, given his appearance, Harry could join either a black or a white regiment, the narrator informs the reader that

> It was as if two paths had suddenly opened before him, and he was forced to choose between them. On one side were strength, courage, enterprise, power of achievement, and memories of a wonderful past. On the other side were weakness, ignorance, poverty, and the proud world's social scorn.[26]

Harry Leroy chooses the black side. When he volunteers, he expressly asks to be assigned to a colored regiment, a request that puzzles the recruiting officer:

> It was a new experience. He had seen colored men with fair complexions anxious to lose their identity with the colored race and pose as white men, but here was a man in the flush of his early manhood, to whom could come dreams of promotion from a simple private to a successful general, deliberately turning his back upon every gilded hope, and dazzling opportunity, to cast his lot with the despised and hated negro.[27]

Scorned by the recruiting officer ("you are the d——d'st fool I ever saw—a man as white as you are turning his back upon his chances for promotion"[28]), Harry Leroy insists upon being identified as a colored man. "Unless I can be assigned to a colored regiment," he declares, "I am not willing to enter the army."[29]

A third hero who refuses to pass is Dr. Frank Latimer.

Though his white ancestry "had effaced all traces of his negro lineage," Dr. Latimer, like the Leroys, insists upon identifying himself as colored. At one point he finds himself (and Dr. Gresham) in the company of an outspokenly racist white physician, Dr. Latrobe, who says all manner of insulting things about blacks, unaware that Latimer considers himself to be a Negro. After hearing Latrobe denigrate blacks and assert that he has a special talent for recognizing even "white niggers," Latimer informs his colleague that, despite appearances, he, too, is black:

> "I am one of them," replied Dr. Latimer, proudly raising his head.
> "You!" exclaimed Dr. Latrobe, with an air of profound astonishment and crimsoning face.
> "Yes," interposed [a white friend of Dr. Latimer], laughing merrily at Dr. Latrobe's discomfiture. "He belongs to that negro race both by blood and choice."[30]

At the end of her novel, Harper arranges for Iola Leroy to marry Dr. Latimer: "kindred hopes and tastes had knit their hearts; grand and noble purposes were lighting up their lives; and they esteemed it a blessed privilege to stand on the threshold of a new era and labor for those who had passed from the old oligarchy of slavery into the new commonwealth of freedom."[31]

Harper never expressly condemns passers; none are among her main characters. Moreover, it is possible to read her as championing the bravery of those who refused to pass as opposed to castigating passers who declined to be heroes. In my view, however, it seems as though Harper is portraying the refusal to pass as a duty and not the gesture of people going beyond the call of duty. She lionizes Iola Leroy and Dr. Latimer not for doing something beyond what can reasonably be expected of good people; she applauds them because they exemplify the racial consciousness that she hopes and expects will become pervasive. Old-fashioned in form— the language is stilted and the plot melodramatic—*Iola Leroy* is alive with racial ideas that remain influential. It accepts the one-drop rule. It cautions against individualistic ambition and lionizes those who sacrifice self-promotion for what Harper sees as the long-term good of blacks as a whole. Harper celebrates black solidarity, champions black racial pride, affirms blacks who recognize racial duties, and lauds African Americans who, though they look white, choose to stand with "their people."

Though disapproval is the dominant motif in the fictional and nonfictional African-American literature on passing, other responses are also discernible. As one of Nella Larsen's* passers observes regarding the ambivalence with which some blacks react to passing: "We disapprove of it and at the same time condone it. It excites our contempt and yet we rather admire it. We shy away from it with an odd kind of revulsion, but we protect it."[32] For some observers, condonation of passing stems from a perception that racial masquerade can constitute

*Nella Larsen (1891–1964) was an important figure in the Harlem Renaissance who wrote one of the most important fictional

an unpleasant but acceptable adaptation to racist mistreatment. In the novel *Plum Bun,* Jessie Redmon Fauset describes a Negro woman who passes occasionally in order to enjoy restaurants and orchestra seats that are customarily reserved for whites. Fauset comments tenderly that the woman "employed her colour very much as she practiced certain winning usages of smile and voice to obtain indulgences which meant much to her and which took nothing from anyone else."[33] "It was with no idea of disclaiming her own that [this woman] sat in orchestra seats . . . denied to coloured patrons," Fauset continued. Rather, the woman's passing stemmed from "a mischievous determination to flout a silly and unjust law."[34]

The nonfiction literature by and about passers is also full of references to passing as a mode of resistance or subversion. The journalist Ray Stannard Baker noted that passing awakened glee among many Negroes because they viewed it as a way of "getting even with the dominant white man."[35] Langston Hughes repeatedly defended passing as a joke on racism.[36] The president of New York's City College, Gregory Howard Williams, relates that his father derived great psychic satisfaction from defying the rules of segregation when he lived in Virginia as the husband of a white woman and the president of a

---

explorations of the phenomenon in American literature, her 1929 novel *Passing*. See George Hutchinson, *In Search of Nella Larsen: A Biography of the Color Line* (2006), and Thadious M. Davis, *Nella Larsen: Novelist of the Harlem Renaissance* (1994).

(supposedly) lily-white chapter of the American Legion.* Williams also relates that his brother got a thrill from romancing white girls who would surely have spurned him had they perceived him to be a Negro. Boasting of one such conquest, Mike Williams declared that after finishing sex he told a girl gleefully, "You just been fucked by a nigger."[37]

The writer Shirlee Taylor Haizlip notes that in Washington, D.C., a "whites only" restaurant in the 1930s hired black people as lookouts to identify White Negroes who were attempting to pass.[38†] In retaliation, a Negro-

---

*According to Williams:

> The nightly crowds huddled at Grandma's relished Dad's stories about how he tricked the white man. Every time the white man was exposed as a fool, laughter rang out through the shack. The victories were small and inconsequential, but I realized the telling and retelling served the valuable purpose of soothing wounded souls. . . .
>
> Dad grew somber when he narrated the story of how, as a teenager, he masqueraded as white and sneaked into Marion, Indiana, thirty miles from Muncie, site of the last hanging in the north, August 7, 1930. He infiltrated the festive white crowd milling around the courthouse lawn where two black teenagers hung long after being beaten, kicked and drug from jail. Four thousand white citizens had stormed the jail and applauded as the youths were killed. Dad shared the horror of Indiana's lynching with Muncie's black community. It was as if he had walked into hell and come out with a report on it.

Life on the Color Line: The True Story of a White Boy Who Discovered He Was Black (1995), pp. 63–64.

†As this story of the restaurant lookouts indicates, passing opened up large possibilities for betrayal, extortion, and revenge. The interesting

owned newspaper published the names of the lookouts.* Perhaps the paper did this only to punish Negroes who aided Jim Crow exclusion and to express no sympathy for passers. On the other hand, the paper's action might have reflected its managers' vicarious pleasure at seeing at least a few Negroes enjoying facilities that racists had hoped to keep exclusively white. An alternative or supplementary sentiment might have been the sense that, regardless of their own motives, passers necessarily dis-

---

thing about this facet of the passing phenomenon is not that outing occasionally occurred but that it appears to have occurred infrequently.

The most horrendous example of outing I have come across stems not from lookouts who fingered Negroes attempting to pass or gays or lesbians attempting to remain closeted, but Jews who betrayed other Jews who were seeking to hide in Hitler's Germany. See Peter Wyden, *Stella* (1992).

*Ray Stannard Baker wrote of blacks creating a "conspiracy of silence" to protect those among them who crossed the line to become white. *Following the Color Line: American Negro Citizenship in the Progressive Era* (1908; reprint 1964), p. 162. A play that dramatizes this point is Regina M. Andrews's *The Man Who Passed: A Play in One Act*. At one point in the play, a Negro barber says to a passer who is returning to Harlem momentarily under cover of darkness:

> You know your own people been pretty good to you, Fred! Ain' none of them spotted you out and hunted you down to tell your Boss Fitzgerald that one of the "Niggers" he hates is working for him, and living right in his own home. It ain't every yellow-faced Negro who can pass for white for fifteen years, hold a white man's job, marry a white woman, and not get caught.

Harlem's Glory: Black Women Writing, 1900–1950, Lorraine Elena Roses and Ruth Elizabeth Randolph, eds. (1996), p. 48.

rupt policies that are intended to bar from positions of authority and privilege *all* persons of African ancestry.

Breaches of the race line accomplished by passing may now appear to be quite minimal. When possibilities for resistance are narrow, however, even the most limited efforts to fool or escape or cheat a repressive social order can be inspiring. This is a point vividly captured by tributes to passers voiced by descendants who appreciate the hard-won benefits that their forbears carved from difficult circumstances through skillful, albeit deceptive, manipulation. Hence, Professor Cheryl I. Harris recalls admiringly her grandmother, a Negro woman who passed for white to get a job in a Chicago department store in the 1930s. "Day in and day out," Harris writes, her grandmother "made herself invisible, then visible, for a price too inconsequential to do more than barely sustain her family."[39]*

Recalling the memory of a White Negro who joined the Washington, D.C., police department during the first decade of the 1900s, Haizlip notes that "the Negro community knew, celebrated, and kept [the passer's]

---

*Similarly, Professor Gabriel Chin memorializes his grandfather, who pretended to be the son of a Chinese immigrant already resident within the United States in order to avoid exclusion under the Chinese Exclusion Act. Professor Chin salutes the "defiance" that made it possible for him to be born in the United States. See Gabriel J. Chin, "Segregation's Last Stronghold: Race Discrimination and the Constitutional Law of Immigration," 46 *UCLA Law Review* 1 (1998). See also Kitty Calavita, "The Paradoxes of Race, Class, Identity, and 'Passing': Enforcing the Chinese Exclusion Acts, 1882–1910," 25 *Law and Social Inquiry* 1 (2000).

secret."[40] Others have responded similarly. Describing his reaction to the realization that some Negroes actually succeeded in pretending to be white, Professor Glenn Loury writes that he enjoyed "imagining my racial brethren surreptitiously infiltrating the citadels of white exclusivity. It allowed me to believe that, despite appearances and the white man's best efforts to the contrary, we blacks were nevertheless present, if unannounced, *everywhere* in American society."[41]*

Opponents of invidious racial discrimination have occasionally deployed passing to confound the administration of the color line. Consider the case of James Hurd, who fought a court order which, if enforced, would have ousted him from his home. He was evicted at the behest of white neighbors who complained that the former owner of his house had signed a contract in which he promised never to sell to or let the house be occupied by a Negro. Hurd raised broad legal issues but also a narrow factual objection. He asserted that the eviction would be improper because he was an Indian and not a Negro.[42] Voicing this defense was none other than Charles Hamilton Houston, the great mentor of the

---

*Professor Judy Scales-Trent voices a similar view:

> [D]on't forget white folks: we see you, we hear you, and we tell our stories. Was that you at a party talking about living in "Coon City"? Little did you know that one of those "coons" was at the party and is writing about you even now. . . . [W]e are everywhere, white folks. Beware.

Notes of a White Black Woman: Race, Color, Community (1995), p. 44.

African-American civil-rights bar in the years prior to *Brown v. Board of Education*. Houston lost on the issue of racial classification (though he ultimately won on the federal constitutional issue).* The important point here, though, is that Houston attempted to use passing—this time passing for Indian—as a vehicle for advancing the cause of racial justice.†

There is a sense in which passing entrenches racial lines of exclusion by reinforcing the norm that certain sectors of society are open only to those who are white or are at least perceived as white. Passing, moreover, has been seen as constituting such a trivial challenge to racial restrictions that some arbiters of the color bar permit

---

*In *Hurd v. Hodge*, 334 U.S. 24 (1948), the Supreme Court held that the federal Constitution prohibited state court judges from evicting Negroes from property they owned that was covered by racially restrictive covenants.

†Professor Christine B. Hickman relates a heartbreaking story about black relatives who bought houses covered by anti-Negro restrictive covenants. Her uncle, Clarence Jones, was a successful Los Angeles attorney whose white neighbors initially left him and his family alone. Ironically, the neighbors' racist stereotype may have prevented them from perceiving Jones as colored. After all, he was a hardworking lawyer whose three daughters attended the University of California at Los Angeles. Not until the wedding of one of the daughters at the family home did the white neighbors become agitated. "As the various guests arrived," Hickman writes, "the neighbors were forced to see what their social training had not let them see before—the Jones family was undeniably black." Soon afterward, white neighbors sued to evict Jones. Jones declined to assert that he was anything but a Negro. Raising arguments on which James Hurd prevailed four years later, Clarence Jones lost his challenge to the constitutionality of

masquerades to go forward as long as passers outwardly obey the rules of white supremacy—that is, pretend actually to be white in return for receiving the privileges that white skin obtains.* With these concerns in mind, the historian Leo Spitzer writes that passing has been

> an action that . . . in no way challenged the ideology of racism or the system in which it was rooted. Indeed, because

---

the state-backed eviction and was forced to move. See *Stone v. Jones,* 152 P.2d 19 (Cal. Ct. App. 1944).

A second uncle passing for white moved into an all-white neighborhood in Detroit, Michigan, in 1956. White neighbors discovered that he was a Negro, perhaps because of the appearance of one of his grandchildren, and demanded that he move. Unlike Clarence Jones, the second uncle attempted to pass. He told reporters that he was half Cherokee and half French Canadian, omitting any mention of his African-American ancestry. The white neighbors, however, rejected his story and increased their pressure, offering to buy the house for two thousand dollars more than he had paid for it and threatening him with mob action in the event that he declined to sell "voluntarily." He soon moved. See "Buyer Beware," *Time,* April 16, 1956, p. 24.

Although Professor Hickman states that "it would not be fair to find fault with [the second uncle's] denial," she admits that she reads about it "with a touch of sadness and a twinge of disappointment because [he] denied who he was and the milling mob did not even listen." See Christine B. Hickman, "The Devil and the One Drop Rule: Racial Categories, African Americans, and the U.S. Census," 95 *Michigan Law Review* 1161, 1169 (1997).

*St. Clair Drake and Horace Cayton found that in the 1940s in Chicago some white people were "willing to overlook a small infusion of Negro blood provided [that] the person who is passing has no social ties with Negroes." *Black Metropolis,* p. 159. Professor James E. DeVries discovered the same phenomenon in researching

individuals responding to marginality through . . . passing could be viewed as either conscious or unwitting accomplices in their own victimization—as persons consenting to the continuing maintenance of existing inequalities and exclusionary ideologies—it is certainly understandable why they often elicited such scathing criticism from their contemporaries.[43]

Passing, however, does pose at least some challenge to racist regimes. That is why they typically try to prevent it. Fleeing bondage by passing may have been an individualistic response to the tyranny of slavery, but it did free human beings and helped to belie the canard that slaves were actually content with their lot. The successful performance of "white man's work" by a passing Negro upset racist claims that blacks are categorically incapable of doing such work. The extent of the disturbance is severely limited by the practical necessity of keeping the passing secret. But under some circumstances a limited disturbance is about all that can be accomplished.

Some critics accuse passers of being complicit in the regimes that they are attempting to escape. Sometimes they are. They may even become loud and fervent bigots

---

his study *Race and Kinship in a Midwestern Town: The Black Experience in Monroe, Michigan, 1900–1915* (1984). According to DeVries, those blacks "who had the physical attributes to pass and who denied their background were, in effect, rewarded with the legal appellation 'white.'" Although many whites realized that the passers "had a 'tainted' lineage, the racist ideology allowed the transition as [the passers] were moving in the right direction." Id., p. 152.

deploying their antiblack prejudice as evidence of authentic whiteness.* But doing so has not typically been a necessary entailment of passing. And it is at least plausible that some passers have attempted to challenge racist practices from their newly acquired positions of racial privilege. Passing does alienate its practitioners from others in the subordinated group. But the same can be said about other strategies that escape the contempt that is routinely heaped upon those who pass. The blacks who fled segregationist oppression in the Jim Crow era could be said to have adopted an "escapist" solution to their plight that distanced them from those they left behind. But criticism on this account is thankfully rare.†

*Harriet Jacobs notes, for example, that one of the most insidious enemies slaves found in her hometown was

> a free colored man, who tried to pass himself off for white . . .
> who was always ready to do any mean work for the sake of
> currying favor with white people. . . . Everybody knew he had
> the blood of a slave father in his veins; but for the sake of pass-
> ing himself off for white, he was ready to kiss the slaveholders'
> feet. How I despised him.

Incidents in the Life of a Slavegirl Written by Herself, Jean Fagan Yellin, ed. (1987, 1861), p. 119.

†Frederick Douglass criticized blacks who migrated to the midwest after the fall of Reconstruction in the South in the 1870s. He thought that it was their duty to stay put despite the privation and violence they faced. He was sharply criticized by other black leaders. In retrospect there is good reason to think that they had the better of the argument. See Nell I. Painter, *Exodusters: Black Migration to Kansas after Reconstruction* (1976, 1986).

Charles W. Chesnutt, himself a "voluntary Negro,"* is one of the few writers who have sympathetically portrayed the White Negro passer. The most notable example of his solicitude is found in his novel *The House Behind the Cedars* (1900). Set in the post-Reconstruction era, this novel tells the story of John and Rena Walden, the children of a white man and his mulatto mistress. John leaves his mother's home in North Carolina with the express purpose of fleeing the constraints imposed upon him by the local knowledge of his racially mixed lineage. He moves to South Carolina, changes his name to John Warwick, passes for white, marries the widow of a Confederate officer, and creates a large, prosperous law practice. Rena stays home with her mother and initially retains her association with their colored neighbors. At John's urging, however, she, too, moves to South Carolina and passes for white. She falls in love with one of John's rich, white clients and draws close to marrying him when, by coincidence, he discovers her racial background and withdraws his proposal of marriage. John counsels her to move to another city and try passing for white once again. Rena refuses and instead rejoins the

---

*Eschewing the option of passing for white, Chesnutt (1858–1932) became the first African-American writer whose craftsmanship was taken seriously by the white literary establishment. Chesnutt dealt with passing repeatedly in his work. See, e.g., *Paul Marchand, F.M.C.* (written in 1921 but published in 1998) and *Mandy Oxendine* (written in 1897 but published in 1997). For more on Chesnutt, see William L. Andrews, *The Literary Career of Charles W. Chesnutt* (1980), and Helen M. Chesnutt, *Charles Waddell Chesnutt: Pioneer of the Color Line* (1952).

colored community in which she was raised. Soon thereafter she tragically dies as a result of efforts to evade a villainous, sexually threatening black man.

In other fictional depictions of passing, it is the person who stays black who attains happiness and the passer who reaps misery. In *The House Behind the Cedars* it is Rena, the sibling who returns to the African-American fold, who suffers. Her brother, by contrast, finds happiness with his racial identity as a white man. Unlike many of the passers portrayed in American fiction, John Warwick evinces no agonized self-doubts about his decision to become white. "I've taken a man's chance in life," he tells his mother, "and have tried to make the most of it; and I haven't felt under any obligation to spoil it by raking up old stories that are best forgotten."[44] Passing is not costless for John. He suffers pain at having to visit his mother's house under cover of darkness. He also suffers from the insecurity that menaces all passers. One of the reasons that he wants his sister to pass and to live with or near him is that he desires the company of at least one person with whom he can be completely open about his racial secret. But in terms of benefits versus costs, there is no question in John's view that passing constituted the right choice for him. "One who had gained so much," he muses, "ought not to complain if he must give a little."[45]

John Warwick's last comment will probably strike some readers as insulting to blacks inasmuch as it suggests that he minimizes the value of his association with African Americans (the "little" thing he believes he must give up) to "gain so much" (public recognition as a white man). Some readers will likely condemn his attitude as a form of self-hatred and racial betrayal. Yet all that makes John "black" is a canon of racial categorization—the one-drop rule—that originated in efforts to perpetuate the subordination of colored people. He should not feel bound to defer to such a rule. He should have the authority to determine for himself with what racial group, if any, he wants to be affiliated. If he chooses to be white, so be it. He looks white. That is what enables him to pass in the first place. Moreover, it is with whites that he obviously feels most at ease. That is what enables him to say that he gives up "little" by leaving the black community of his childhood and joining the white community of his adulthood. If he were giving up what he considered to be "too much" he would presumably decline to pass.

That racial passing remains a touchy subject is shown by the vehemence with which it is often still denounced.* "Trying to forgive Blacks who pass is difficult," Profes-

---

*Passing of various sorts remains controversial. Heated debate surrounded Secretary of State Madeleine Albright when journalists reported that some of her ancestors were Jews who had perished in the Holocaust. Some charged that she, a practicing Episcopalian, had misleadingly denied knowledge of those facts to maintain distance from her Jewish roots. See Michael Dobbs, *Madeleine Albright: A Twentieth-Century Odyssey* (2000), pp. 377–95, and Peter Margulies, "The Identity Question, Madeleine Albright's Past and Me: Insights from Jewish and African-American Law and Literature," 17 *Loyola of Los Angeles Entertainment Law Review* 595 (1997). And, of course, passing with respect to sexual orientation has sparked several debates central to recent struggles for gay and lesbian liberation. Examples include disputes over the morality of outing (see Larry Gross, *Contested Closets: The Politics and Ethics of Outing* [1993])

sor Ronald E. Hall writes. "I feel that by passing, they have cursed the memory of every dark skinned person on their family tree."[46] Similarly, Professor Adrian Piper remarks that "Trying to forgive . . . those of my relatives who have chosen to pass for white has been one of the most difficult ethical challenges of my life."[47] One might have thought that racial passing and anxieties about it would have been rendered marginal by now, given substantial declines in the intensity and power of antiblack feelings and practices. Being perceived as black no longer bars one absolutely from most of society's attractive opportunities. But for some observers, the specter of racial disunity, racial disloyalty, and even racial dissolution loom larger now precisely because African Americans have more choice than ever before regarding whom to marry, where to live, or what school to attend. With more choices, larger numbers of blacks have more opportunity to distance themselves physically, socially, and psychologically from other blacks.* The prospect of new modes of "passing" in which, regardless of hue,

---

and the federal government's "don't ask, don't tell" policy, which effectively demands passing as a requirement for military service by lesbians and gays (see Janet Halley, *Don't: A Reader's Guide to the Military's Anti-Gay Policy* [1995]).

*Professor John O. Calmore writes, "Even dark-skinned, nappy-headed African Americans like me can pass sociologically and culturally if we have the right history of socialization, the right credentials, a respectable job, an affluent income, and a proper street address or zip code." "Dismantling the Master's House: Essays in Memory of Trina Grillo: Random Notes of an Integration Warrior," 81 *Minnesota Law Review* 1441 (1997).

Negroes become so-called Oreos—black on the outside but white on the inside—has played a role in prompting some African Americans to intensify their commitment to group solidarity. These advocates of black communitarianism seek to instill a heightened sense of racial obligation into African Americans, eschew assimilation into "mainstream" (i.e., "white") society, and champion the strengthening of a separate black solidarity, asserting unapologetically that blacks ought to prefer one another to nonblack Others. A broad array of African Americans have adopted these ideological premises. They loathe passers. They disparage blacks who marry whites. They oppose interracial adoptions. They resist changes in verbal formulations or census classifications that would enable those now deemed to be "black" to identify themselves differently (for instance, as a "multiracial" person). They see these activities as "escapist," "inauthentic," "fraudulent" desertions that are tantamount to "selling out."

In my view, people ought to be permitted presumptively to enter and exit racial categories at their choosing, even if the choices made clash with conventional understandings of racial classification. If a person who is "black" under the one-drop rule identifies herself as "white," that self-identification should ordinarily conclude the matter of racial classification. Except for circumstances to which I shall soon turn, this hypothesized passer should be deemed white without social disapproval.

Are there circumstances, however, in which it is defensible to subordinate an individual's preference for adopting this or that racial identity to other considerations? The answer is yes. An individual ought to be permitted *presumptively* to enter and exit racial categories freely. But that presumption is overcome when there is a clear and convincing basis for discouraging a particular instance of individual choice. Here the politics of sexual orientation again offer useful lessons.

Within gay and lesbian communities there exists a strong presumption in favor of protecting from exposure the secret sexual predilections of closeted individuals— that is, people who are widely perceived as "straight" (heterosexual) though they are in fact "queer" (homosexual). In the 1980s, however, certain gay and lesbian activists began to challenge the sanctity of the closet by revealing, under special circumstances, the orientation of individuals who were passing as straight. There are two main circumstances in which the "outing" of closeted figures has been justified.* One involves figures who are deemed to have betrayed the gay or lesbian community by actively supporting individuals, organizations, or policies that expressly attack those communities. The most striking example is Terry Dolan, a founder and leader of

---

*"Outing" refers to the practice of revealing information about a person that he or she seeks to keep hidden. The principal source on which I have relied in constructing my comparison of outing with respect to race and outing with respect to sexual orientation is Larry Gross, *Contested Closets: The Politics and Ethics of Outing* (1993). See also Richard Mohr, *Gay Ideas: Outing and Other Controversies* (1992); Claudia Mills, "Passing: The Ethics of Pretending to Be What You Are Not," 25 *Social Theory and Practice* 29 (1999).

the National Conservative Political Action Committee (NCPAC), which unapologetically supported politicians who were overtly antigay. In this context, outing functions as a penalty for hypocrisy* and a punishment meant to dissuade closeted gays from reaping the benefits of gay-lesbian communal life, including companionship and secrecy, while simultaneously aiding in the suppression of gay-lesbian communal life.

The other main circumstance in which outing has been justified involves publicizing the sexual orientation of especially powerful, prestigious, or well-known individuals. Examples in this category include Rock Hudson, the movie star; David Geffen, the music and film mogul; Merv Griffin, the television entrepreneur; and Jodie Foster, the actress. The rationale for outing in this context is that doing so furthers the deconstruction of negative stereotypes of gays and lesbians by showing people that among the individuals they have liked and admired are some who just happen to be queer. Proponents of outing for this purpose argue that for gay and lesbian public figures to stay within the closet constitutes a betrayal of gay or lesbian communities by depriving them of visibility and of role models who can be emulated and admired by the public at large, straights and queers alike.† While

---

*Defending the outing of closeted gay politicians who support antigay policies, Congressman Barney Frank remarks: "There's a right to privacy but not to hypocrisy." Quoted in Gross, *Contested Closets*, p. 3.

†"Every [gay] star who is in the public eye does the [gay] community a disservice by pretending to straight. By their silence, they are

deferring to individual choice in the ordinary case, proponents of outing are willing in the unusual case to use a type of coercion—the force of exposure—to advance communal interests even at the expense of the privacy of individuals who would have preferred to remain closeted.

In the case of the White Negro passer, there are similarly special circumstances in which it might be justifiable to "out" someone. Imagine a White Negro analogue to Terry Dolan—that is, a closeted Negro who actively supports anti-Negro politicians. Some will likely question whether the analogy is apposite. A closeted gay or lesbian is a person who seeks to embrace two societies: straight society for purposes of public acknowledgment and queer society for purposes of private pleasure. The White Negro who seeks to pass permanently, however, seeks a place not in white *and* black society but only in

---

reinforcing the idea that America is straight. Their silence alone is treason." Vito Russo quoted in Larry Bush, "Naming Gay Names," *Village Voice,* April 27, 1982.

According to Gabriel Rotello, the former editor of *OutWeek:* "It's taken for granted that other minorities deserve to have role models, so why not gays?" See Dirk Johnson, "Privacy vs. the Pursuit of Gay Rights," *New York Times,* March 27, 1990. A similar view is expressed by another former editor at *OutWeek,* Michelangelo Signorile. "How can we ever convince the public that homosexuality is normal unless we show the public who is gay?" he asks. See John P. Elwood, "Outing, Privacy, and the First Amendment," 102 *Yale Law Journal* 747, 748, n. 5 (1993). "The language of outing is the language of community and accountability, of the condemnation of passing and the demand for public affirmation of gay identity by the legion of closeted stars and athletes, fashion designers and fashion plates, politicians and tycoons." Gross, *Contested Closets,* p. 35.

the former; he abandons his citizenship in Black America. There have been White Negroes, however, who have passed on merely a temporary or partial basis—at work they have been white; at play they have been black. A White Negro engaged in temporary passing who aided expressly anti-Negro forces would be analogous to Terry Dolan. Fortunately, the number of such persons is probably small; I know of none.

A more likely scenario is the case of the White Negro passer who is the target of outing because of his celebrity or prestige. Outing in this instance might be done not as punishment but as a way of forcibly associating the passer with Black America. The aim would be to capitalize on his social standing for the sake of the black image in the popular mind. Imagine it was discovered, for example, that the biological parents of Bill Gates (the founder of Microsoft) and Roger D. Kornberg (the winner of the 2006 Nobel Prize for Chemistry) were black. A racial outer might argue that publicizing this information is justified because of the good it would do in eroding racial superstitions that continue to menace black Americans—namely, the myth of Negro incompetence.

I do not reject categorically the prospect of outing a White Negro passer. Under certain circumstances doing so would be justifiable. Those circumstances, however, are unlikely to surface. In the context of sexual orientation, outing has rightly been used as a weapon against closeted gay "sellouts." But, as mentioned above, there exist few, if any, racial analogues to Terry Dolan. The principal reason for this has to do with the status of gays as a group versus blacks as a group. Gays are substantially more vulnerable to prejudice than blacks. A plethora of federal and state laws expressly discriminate against gays and lesbians. The armed forces expressly prohibit openly queer individuals from service. Except in Massachusetts, same-sex couples are excluded from legally recognized marriage. Several states discourage or prohibit gay or lesbian adults from adopting children. Such invidious discriminations on a racial basis are now unthinkable. A black American who is "straight" can be a serious contender for the presidency; an openly gay or lesbian American cannot, regardless of his or her race. In many cases politicians can support invidious discrimination based on sexual orientation and expect to pay only a marginal electoral price for doing so; indeed, in some instances by doing so they can reap substantial electoral benefit. By contrast, open expression of racial prejudice is politically and socially suicidal. The civil-rights revolution closed the door to racial analogues to Terry Dolan by marginalizing the openly racist politics on which such figures would have fed.*

There is an additional reason it is unlikely that the special circumstances that justify outing in the context of closeted gays or lesbians will obtain in the context of White Negro passers. A key aim of the campaign to coax or force gays and lesbians out of the closet was to make

---

*I am not saying that racist appeals are a thing of the past in American electoral politics. I am saying that such appeals are no longer *openly* made by major politicians. The delegitimation of frank racism requires those who make racist appeals to do so indirectly, under the cover of coded language. See Tali Mendelberg, *The Race Card: Campaign Strategy, Implicit Messages, and the Norm of Equality* (2001).

them visible. With blacks, the situation is far different. The uniform of skin color makes most blacks highly visible, thus obviating any need to bring them "out" to one another and the public in general. It has often been claimed that the visibility of blacks is a major encumbrance and that, especially in comparison with gays and lesbians, blacks are disadvantaged by their inability to become invisible. As Professor Bruce Ackerman has argued, however, the exact opposite is true.* Far from being an unequivocal benefit, the invisibility of closeted gays has been a daunting obstacle confronting the gay-lesbian liberation movement. After all, invisibility greatly increases the difficulty of identifying, communicating with, and organizing fellow gays and lesbians.

In the end, then, my view of racial "outing" is consonant with my view of indicting individuals for "selling out." If one insists upon maintaining a collective identity for Black Americans, one must allow for the prospect of

---

*"Compare the problem faced by black political organizers with the one confronting organizers of the homosexual community. As a member of an anonymous group, each homosexual can seek to minimize the personal harm due to prejudice by keeping his or her sexual preferences a tightly held secret. Although this is hardly a satisfactory response, secrecy does enable homosexuals to 'exit' from prejudices in a way that blacks cannot. This means that a homosexual group must confront an organizational problem that does not arise for its black counterpart: somehow the group must induce each anonymous homosexual to reveal his or her sexual preference to the larger public and to bear the private costs this public declaration may involve." Bruce Ackerman, "Beyond Carolene Products," 98 *Harvard Law Review* 713, 730–31 (1985).

coercion in defense of the group. Properly deploying coercion is so hazardous, however, that, except in extraordinary circumstances, I strongly advise abjuring it even for purposes of solidarity or collective advancement. Rather than chaining people forever to the racial status into which they were born, we should try to both eradicate the deprivations that have often impelled people to want to pass *and* protect individuals' capacity for racial self-determination, including their ability to revise racial identities.

EPILOGUE

"This isn't selling out, it's selling up."

Jesse Jackson (2000)*

This book stems, to a substantial degree, from two personal experiences. One is being called a sellout. The other is my encounters with black students at Harvard Law School who fear that appellation.

I have been called a sellout on numerous occasions. The first arose when, as a recent law-school graduate, I defended one of the great white liberals of the twentieth century, Jack Greenberg, against attacks by those who objected to his long-standing leadership of the NAACP Legal Defense Fund and his role as a teacher of race-relations law.[1] I was denounced as a sellout several years later when I challenged certain axioms embraced by proponents of the emerging critical-race-theory movement. I questioned whether it had been persuasively demonstrated that racial-minority scholars had been unfairly treated by white scholars in the law-review literature, whether racial-minority scholars really do have a

---

*Reverend Jackson made this remark in defense of Bob Johnson, the founder of Black Entertainment Television (BET), when Johnson was harshly criticized for selling the network he founded to a predominantly white conglomerate. See Teresa Wiltz, "But Has the Network Sold a Bit of Its Soul?," *Washington Post*, Nov. 4, 2000.

special—racially determined—insight into race-relations law, and whether, as a matter of scholarly procedure, racial-minority status should be seen as an intellectual credential.[2] For pressing such questions, I was rebuked as a treacherous Tonto in blackface who was mainly concerned with securing the esteem of whites, particularly white colleagues who would assess me for purposes of tenure.[3] A while later I was again called a sellout, this time by detractors who objected to my campaign against race matching—the policy of preferring, or even requiring, same-race adoption—and my defense of interracial dating and marriage.*

These episodes, however, were nothing compared with the denunciations I received in the aftermath of writing *Nigger: The Strange Career of a Troublesome Word* (2003). That book explored the etymology of the N-word, traced its racist history, examined how judges and juries have grappled with it in legal disputes, and described how it has figured in numerous social controversies. I argued that the infamous N-word, like all words, takes its meaning from the context in which it is used. Presumptively a racist insult, it can also be a term of endearment, a gesture of black solidarity, and even a weapon of

---

*During a reading of my book *Interracial Intimacies: Sex, Marriage, Identity, and Adoption* (2003) at a bookstore in Washington, D.C., a disgruntled member of the audience turned to her neighbor and began to chastise me for betraying the race. She said to him that she just knew that I was married to a white woman. He replied that he was quite sure that that was not the case. She persisted, asserting that, given my views, I *must* be married to a white woman. At that point, her neighbor, a black man, informed the woman that he was better informed than she inasmuch as his daughter was my wife!

antiracist propaganda. While I expressed opposition to racist uses of the word by anyone regardless of race, I also defended justifiable uses of the word by anyone, regardless of race. For these views, and especially for putting "nigger" into the highly publicized title of the book, I became the target of some rough verbal blows, the most outlandish of which were thrown in the pages of the Internet publication the Black Commentator. According to Professor Martin Kilson, the first black tenured professor at Harvard University, my "core purpose . . . was to assist White Americans in feeling comfortable with using the epithet 'nigger.'"[4] I wrote a rebuttal to Professor Kilson's article that prompted additional lashings. Glen Ford and Peter Gamble, writing on behalf of an entity with the wonderfully apt title the Council on Black Internal Affairs,* castigated me as a "racial free-loader" whom they "despise[d]." I have, they asserted, "opportunistically used [my] status as a well-known Black public intellectual to reap profit and a perverse sort of fame through . . . 'a cold indifference to the typical sensibilities of African-American citizens.'" For these purported infractions they hoped that I would be punished:

> We don't care how Kennedy makes his money—unless it is by giving aid and comfort to racists. We believe Kennedy's

*The most significant accomplishment of the Council thus far is its publication of a remarkable volume: *The American Directory of Certified Uncle Toms: Being a Review of the History, Antics, and Attitudes of Handkerchief Heads, Aunt Jemimas, Head Negroes in Charge, and House Negroes Against the Freedom Aims of the Black Race* (2002).

calculated maneuvers are more harmful than the crimes of common felons. . . . He needs to wander in the wilderness for five or ten years, to do penance for his crime, followed by additional years of atonement. . . . Repudiate Randall Kennedy, *loudly,* wherever and whenever he pops up, and you will have neutered him, and made others consider taking another path.[5]

Several years later, the N-word again complicated my life when I testified as an expert witness for the defense in an assault case stemming from the brutal beating of a black man. The altercation reportedly began with the assailant, a white man, saying to the black man, "Whatup, nigga?" The defense contended that the assailant was not using the term as a racial insult but was using it the way it is often used by young men deeply influenced by hip-hop culture. I was asked to repeat on the witness stand what I had written in my book: that "nigga" and its variants ("nigger," "nigguh," etc.), while presumptively racial insults, can signal other meanings depending on the circumstances. I was not asked to comment on the facts of the case at hand but only on the chameleonlike nature of the N-word.*

After I testified, a commentator in the Black Commentator called me "a very cheap whore."† "Kennedy obvi-

---

*For an interesting comparison, see David Wilkins, "Race, Ethics, and the First Amendment: Should a Black Lawyer Represent the Ku Klux Klan?" 63 *George Washington Law Review* 1030 (1995).
†The reference to "cheap" alludes to the fact, disclosed by the defendant's attorney, that I received neither a fee nor expenses for my testimony. I acted pro bono mainly because of the long prison term at stake. I had no objection to hate-crime legislation or a finding of guilt

ously doesn't care about black people," she asserted. "He is an opportunistic self-hater with all of the establishment's top credentials, a very dangerous enemy indeed."[6]

Knowing of my confrontations with this sort of vituperation, supporters have praised me for being "brave." The fact is, however, that I have not felt threatened by any ideological enemies. At no point have I felt that I was putting myself into serious jeopardy because of something I have had in mind to write. That is largely because I am unusually well protected. I have long been a tenured professor at a great university that puts a premium on cultivating an environment in which intellectual freedom flourishes. So my livelihood has not been threatened. And the prospect of interference from governmental authorities has been practically nonexistent.

The security that I happily enjoy is nourished by key ingredients that sustain our society's vibrancy. Among these are limitations, including self-restraints, on the deployment of power. In assessing the word "sellout" I

---

in this instance. I simply wanted the jury to come to an appropriate decision based on the facts of *this* case and not based on the notion, embraced by some, that the word "nigger" spoken by a white person is invariably a sign of racial animus. The jury convicted the defendant of committing a hate crime. I have no reason to doubt its judgment. See Corey Kilgannon, "Bat-Wielding Attacker Gets 15 Years for Hate Crime," *New York Times,* July 18, 2006; Corey Kilgannon, "Epithet 'Has Many Meanings,' A Harvard Professor Testifies," *New York Times,* June 8, 2006.

Regarding the matter of fees, one can only imagine what would have been said about me had I been paid.

am assessing the deployment of a certain type of power—
rhetorical power. In the context of our discussion, "sellout" is a stigmatizing weapon typically wielded by people
who face and are attempting to overcome unjust racial
discrimination. For that reason, their rhetorical practices
are often ignored by sympathetic onlookers. That is a
mistake. Examining the deployment of power by anyone, including the relatively disempowered, is a useful
endeavor because victims in one setting often become
victimizers in another. That is why it is important to
attend critically not only to the conduct of the strong, the
established, the oppressor, but also to the conduct of the
weak, the dissident, the oppressed.

There is a second personal experience closely related
to the writing of this book. It involves my interactions for
a bit over twenty years with black students and alumni at
Harvard Law School. Annually the school's Black Law
Students Association (BLSA) sponsors two events that I
usually attend. One is a gathering at the beginning of
each school year to which all of the black professors are
invited to speak to the incoming class of black law students. The other is a weekend conference in the spring
aimed at drawing alumni back to campus. At both, fear
of selling out is thick in the air. At the gathering in the
fall, there is much exhortation about the racial obligation
to "give back" to the black community and to avoid
"forgetting where you come from." And one can be certain that references, usually several, will be made to a
statement that has now become iconic within the black
bar—the claim, attributed to Charles Hamilton Hous-

ton, that "a lawyer's either a social engineer or he's a parasite on society."[7]* At the spring conference, there are always panels featuring alumni who insist that, despite their ensconcement in the higher echelons of the nation's preeminent law firms or businesses, they nonetheless make sure to "give back," to "stay black," to pay their racial dues. Regardless of the stated themes of the spring conferences, an implicit subtheme earnestly voiced in practically all of them is that the students nearing graduation will not sell out and that the alumni participants have not sold out. Onlooking skeptics resist these efforts at absolution, insisting that everyone ought to be paying much more in racial dues. Some will even contend that proper respect for racial obligation entails giving up affluence and committing oneself root-and-branch to those blacks who are truly disadvantaged. These skeptics often end their stern upbraidings with a flourish, accusing the black middle class of sedating the black masses in

*Charles Hamilton Houston (1895–1950) was an outstanding civil-rights attorney and legal academic. A leading figure at the Howard University School of Law, he trained and inspired a remarkable cadre of attorneys, including Oliver Hill, Spottswood Robinson, and Thurgood Marshall. See Genna Rae McNeil, *Groundwork: Charles Hamilton Houston and the Struggle for Civil Rights* (1983). Professor Kenneth Mack notes that there exists no writing in which Houston says expressly what has now become the most well-known statement attributed to him. The statement is one that former students Thurgood Marshall and William Hastie recall him making. For a richly detailed, deeply informed interpretation of Houston and his colleagues, see Kenneth Mack, "Rethinking Civil Rights Lawyering and Politics in the Era Before Brown," 115 *Yale Law Journal* 256 (2005).

exchange for tokenism—a few high governmental posts
for safe Negroes, a handful of top corporate posts for
blacks who are willing to commit the same antisocial acts
that white bosses commit, an array of affirmative-action
slots.[8]

Most people in the audience silently dismiss the
demand for maximalist sacrifice. They have come to
Harvard because they want enhanced access to upward
mobility. But the maximalist message, supplemented by
the other talk stressing racial obligation, does have consequences. For an appreciable number of students, it
induces guilt, making them embarrassed about pursuits
for which they ought not feel ashamed. I see this effect
when I ask them where they are spending the summer
after their first or second year of law school or where
they are going for their initial full-time lawyering job.
They lower their voices and indicate apologetically that
they are working for this or that firm but that they intend to do so only briefly to pay off loans or address
some other exigency. When I explore the issue further it
becomes clear that they feel compelled to justify themselves in this way to avoid being labeled a sellout by peers
or, perhaps more important, by themselves. Concern
over their misplaced angst played a large role in prompting me to think about the idea of the sellout in black
American life.

I tell these students that they should not permit an
inflated conception of racial obligation to weigh them
down. I tell them that they should pursue happiness
untrammeled by excessive racial dues. I tell them that if

civil-rights law or some similar enterprise is their passion, then they should certainly pursue it—not as an exercise in martyrdom but as a fulfilling expression of what they most want to do with their talents. I also tell them that if they want to become the managing partner of Cravath, Swaine & Moore (or any other citadel of the Establishment), that is what they should seek to accomplish, and that if this is what they really want then they must go after that goal wholeheartedly, for otherwise they have no chance for success. I tell them that there is nothing wrong with such an ambition and that pursuing such a goal does not represent a betrayal of previous struggles for racial justice. Such struggles were waged (or should have been waged) precisely to enable blacks to construct decent lives according to their own designs, free of racial restrictions. I tell the students to be careful about using or being used by the haunting specter of "the sellout." It is more of a bane than a benefit to black folks' ongoing struggle for advancement.

Acknowledgments

I wrote this book in the aftermath of a great personal tragedy: the death of my darling wife, Dr. Yvedt Lové Matory. Many people have helped me to cope with this painful loss. None have been more supportive than our valiant children: Henry William Kennedy, Rachel Elizabeth Lové Kennedy, and Thaddeus James Kennedy. My mother, Rachel Spann Kennedy, and my father-in-law, Dr. William Matory, have also been unstinting in their encouragement.

For constant, bracing, loving friendship I thank William and Ali Achtmeyer, the Acree clan, Janice Allen, Dave Barcomb, Nelson Costa, Leslie Creutzfelt, Lynne Dichter, Hillary Fabre, Rosita and Steven Fine, Eric Foner, Clint and Kim Furnald, Lynne Garofola, Robert and Kathy Gilbert, Lani Guinier, Cynthia Harmon, Elizabeth Karasik, Altomease Kennedy, Victoria and Nordstrom Knox, Tamsin Knox, John and Maggie Lamb, Sanford and Cynthia Levinson, Ken Mack, Polly and Kevin Maroni, Randy and Bunmi Matory, Elizabeth Matory, Bill and Kea Matory, Rita Matory, Mac and Wendy McCorkle, Ann and Colin McNay, Stephanie Meilman, Carol Oja, Carolyn and Bob Osteen, Tina and Alvin Poussaint, Paul and Rita Rampell, Celia Sandel, Kiku and Michael Sandel, Megan Schaefer-Curran, Benjamin Sears, Martha and Joe Singer, Olivia Moorehead-Slaughter, Wick and Margaret Sollers, Aviam Soifer, the Spann clan, David Slye, Phyllis Slye, Laurie Turner, Roger Volk, David and Anne Marie Wilkins, Martin J. Wohl, and Kent Yucel.

Harvard Law School is my wonderful intellectual home. My colleagues and students have provided me with inspiration and counsel for which I am deeply grateful. The school's extraordinary dean, Elena Kagan, has played a major role in sustaining my spirits. Her steadfast support has been crucial. Indispensable, too, have been the labors on my behalf undertaken by the expert and friendly stewards of the reference desk at the Harvard Law School Library: Janet Katz, Michael Jimenez, Karen Storin Linitz, Deanna Barmakian, June Casey, Martin Hollick, Elizabeth Lambert, Naomi Ronen, Terry Swanlund, and Josh Kanter.

I have profited from the comments of scores of readers and listeners including Rick Banks, Martin Bell, Taj Clayton, Sabrina Charles, Devon Carbado, Russell Robinson, David Dolinko, and Eddie Glaude. I would similarly like to thank audiences at the State of Black Men in America Conference sponsored by the Princeton University Black Men's Awareness Group, the UCLA Law School workshop, the Law and Philosophy Seminar at the University of Chicago School of Law, the Pastora San Juan Cafferty Lecture at the University of Chicago School of Social Services Administration, the 2006 Martin Luther King, Jr., Convocation at Carleton College, a seminar at the William S. Richardson School of Law at the University of Hawaii, where I had the honor of serving as the Frank Boas Visiting Professor, and my inaugural lecture as the Michael R. Klein Professor of Law at Harvard University—an event graced by the presence of the Klein family.

Professors Tommie Shelby and Valerie Smith were especially generous in their reading of the manuscript and sharing of ideas.

Near the completion of this project, my friend, mentor, and teacher John F. McCune passed away. At St. Albans School, Mr. McCune—"Gentleman Jack"—introduced me to the joys of scholarship, especially historiographical inquiry. I shall always admire him.

Finally, I'd like to acknowledge again the person to whom this book is dedicated—my brother, Judge Henry H. Kennedy, Jr. He has been with me every step of the way. Being the beneficiary of his wisdom, good humor, and care has indeed been a blessing.

Notes

PREFACE

1. See Mancur Olson, *The Logic of Collective Action: Public Goods and the Theory of Groups* (1965, 1971); Dennis Chong, *Collective Action and the Civil Rights Movement* (1991); Eric A. Posner, "The Regulation of Groups: The Influence of Legal and Nonlegal Sanctions on Collective Action," 63 *University of Chicago Law Review* 133 (1996).
2. Cf. Judith Shklar, "The Ambiguities of Betrayal," in *Ordinary Vices* (1989); Carl J. Friedrich, *The Pathology of Politics: Violence, Betrayal, Corruption, Secrecy, and Propaganda* (1972), pp. 81–94.
3. Kevin Merida and Michael A. Fletcher, "Supreme Discomfort," *Washington Post Magazine*, Aug. 4, 2002.
4. Ibid.
5. See Nell I. Painter, "Martin R. Delany: Elitism and Black Nationalism," in Leon Litwack and August Meier, eds., *Black Leaders of the Nineteenth Century* (1988).
6. Peter Beinart, "Black Like Me," *The New Republic*, Feb. 5, 2007.
7. Eric Deggans, "Obama Takes up Race Issue," *St. Petersburg Times*, Aug. 11, 2007.
8. Jill Nelson, *Volunteer Slavery: My Authentic Negro Experience* (1993), p. 56.

One WHO IS "BLACK"?

1. See cbsnews.com/stories/2007/02/09/60minutes.

2. See Barack Obama, *Dreams from My Father: A Story of Race and Inheritance* (1995, 2004); Michael Barone and Richard E. Cohen, *The Almanac of American Politics 2006* (2006), pp. 557–60; *CQ's Politics in America 2006: The 109th Congress,* Jackie Koszczuk and H. Amy Stern, eds. (2006), pp. 329–30; William Finnegan, "The Candidate," *The New Yorker,* May 31, 2004.

3. See Debra J. Dickerson, "Colorblind," Salon.com.2007/01/22. See also Stanley Crouch, "What Obama Isn't: Black Like Me," New York *Daily News,* Nov. 2, 2006. For articles canvassing the debate generated by the questioning of Obama's racial standing, see Marjorie Valbrun, "Black Like Me?," *Washington Post,* Feb. 16, 2007; "The Obama Card," *Los Angeles Times,* Feb. 13, 2007; Satta Sarmah, "Is Obama Black Enough?," cjrdaily.org, Feb. 15, 2007; Annette John-Hall, "'Black Enough'? Enough's Enough," philly.com, March 30, 2007; Brent Staples, "Decoding the Debate over the Blackness of Barack Obama," *New York Times,* Feb. 11, 2007; Rachel L. Swarns, "So Far, Obama Can't Take Black Vote for Granted," *New York Times,* Feb. 2, 2007.

4. cbsnews.com/stories/2007/02/09/60minutes.

5. W. E. B. DuBois, *Dusk of Dawn: An Essay Toward an Autobiography of a Race Concept* (1940; 1992), p. 153.

6. On the history and administration of the one-drop rule, see F. James Davis, *Who Is Black? One Nation's Definition* (1991); Christine B. Hickman, "The Devil and the One Drop Rule: Racial Categories, African Americans and the U.S. Census," 95 *Michigan Law Review* 1161 (1997); Daniel J. Sharfstein, "Crossing the Color Line: Racial Migration and the One-Drop Rule, 1600–1860," 91 *Minnesota Law Review* 592 (2007).

7. Quoted in Randall Kennedy, *Interracial Intimacies: Sex, Marriage, Identity, and Adoption* (2003), p. 298.

8. Hickman, p. 1166. See also Tanya Kateri Hernandez, "'Mul-

tiracial' Discourse: Racial Classifications in an Era of Color-Blind Jurisprudence," 57 *Maryland Law Review* 98 (1998), pp. 121–28.

9. Gilbert Stephenson, *Race Distinctions in American Law* (1910), p. 15; Richard B. Sherman, "'The Last Stand': The Fight for Racial Integrity in Virginia in the 1920s," 54 *Journal of Southern History* 1 (1988).

10. See Willard B. Gatewood, *Aristocrats of Color: The Black Elite, 1880–1920* (1990), pp. 149–81; Joel Williamson, *New People: Miscegenation and Mulattoes in the United States* (1995); Kathy Russell, Midge Wilson, and Ronald Hall, *The Color Complex: The Politics of Skin Color Among African Americans* (1992); Trina Jones, "Shades of Brown: The Law of Skin Color," 49 *Duke Law Journal* 1487 (2000).

11. Michael P. Johnson and James L. Roark, *Black Masters: A Free Family of Color in the Old South* (1984), p. xi.

12. Bureau of the Census, U.S. Dept. of Commerce, *Seventh Census of the United States: 1850* (1853), p. xxii; Hickman, p. 1185.

13. Hickman, p. 1185.

14. Bureau of the Census, U.S. Dept. of Commerce, *Negro Population of the United States, 1790–1915*, William Loren Katz, ed. (1968), p. 207.

15. See generally Edward Byron Reuter, *The Mulatto in the United States* (1918); Joel Williamson, *New People: Miscegenation and Mulattoes in the United States* (1995); Russell et al., *The Color Complex*; Jones, "Shades of Brown."

16. See Howard E. Freeman, J. Michael Ross, David Armor, and Thomas F. Pettigrew, "Color Gradation and Attitudes Among Middle-Income Negroes," 31 *American Sociological Review* 365 (1966), describing a variant of the saying in the text as "an oft-repeated adage among color-sensitive Negroes in the United States."

17. Bureau of the Census, U.S. Dept. of Commerce, *Fourteenth Census of the United States: 1920* (1923), p. 10.

18. Williamson, p. 114.

19. See Stephen Jay Gould, *The Mismeasure of Man* (1981); John S. Haller, Jr., *Outcasts from Evolution: Scientific Attitudes of Racial Inferiority, 1859–1900* (1971); William Stanton, *The Leopard's Spots: Scientific Attitudes Toward Race in America, 1815–59* (1960); Winthrop D. Jordan, *White over Black: American Attitudes Toward the Negro, 1550–1812* (1968).

20. *Hudgins v. Wright,* 11 Va. 134 (1806).

21. Robert Westley, "First-time Encounters: 'Passing' Revisited and Demystification as a Critical Practice," 18 *Yale Law & Policy Review* 297, 348 (2000). See also Gerald Horne, *The Color of Fascism: Lawrence Dennis, Racial Passing, and the Rise of Right-Wing Extremism in the United States* (2006), p. 6.

22. Sharfstein, "Crossing the Color Line," p. 595.

23. 1 N.C. 188 (1802).

24. *Bennett v. Bennett,* 10 S.E.2d 23 (1940).

25. *State v. Cantey,* 20 S.C.L. 614 (1835).

26. Professor Valerie Smith in letter to Randall Kennedy, June 10, 2007. See also Orlando Patterson, "The New Black Nativism," *Time,* Feb. 8, 2007.

27. See, e.g., Adrian Piper, "Passing for White, Passing for Black," in *Out of Order, Out of Sight, volume I: Selected Essays in Meta-Art, 1968–1992* (1996); Judy Scales-Trent, *Notes of a White Black Woman: Race, Color, Community* (1995).

28. See, generally, Kimberly McClain DaCosta, *Making Multiracials: State, Family, and Market in the Redrawing of the Color Line* (2007).

29. See "Tiger Woods Says He Is More Than Black," *Jet,* May 12, 1997; Salim Muwakkil, "Deconstructing Blackness," *In These Times,* June 16, 1997; Gary Kamiya, "Cablinasian Like Me," salon.com, April 30, 1997.

30. See Kennedy, pp. 333–34. See also Luther Wright, Jr., "Who's Black, Who's White, and Who Cares: Reconceptualizing the United States's Definition of Race and Racial Classifications," 48 *Vanderbilt Law Review* 513 (1995). Jay Mathews, "Blue-Eyed Official Ran as Black, Faces Recall," *Washington Post,* May 6, 1984.

31. Cited in Frank N. Sweet, "Features of Today's One-drop Rule," backintyme.com, March 1, 2005.

32. Ibid.

33. Ibid.

34. See Kennedy, pp. 334–38; Wright, "Who's Black, Who's White." See also *Malone v. Malone,* Supreme Judicial Court for Suffolk County, No. 88–339, July 25, 1989, Associate Justice Herbert P. Wilkins presiding.

Two THE IDEA OF THE SELLOUT IN
BLACK AMERICAN HISTORY

1. David Walker, *Appeal . . . to the Coloured Citizens of the World,* edited with an introduction and annotations by Peter P. Hinks (2000), p. 32.

2. Ibid., p. 13.

3. Ibid., p. 25.

4. Ibid., p. 29.

5. Darold D. Wax, "'The Great Risque We Run': The Aftermath of Slave Rebellion at Stono, South Carolina, 1739–1745," 67 *Journal of Negro History* 136, 141 (1982).

6. See Douglas R. Egerton, *Gabriel's Rebellion: The Virginia Slave Conspiracies of 1800 and 1802* (1993), pp. 67–72.

7. Ibid., pp. 105–7.

8. *A Documentary History of the Negro People in the United States,* Herbert Aptheker, ed. (1951, 1990), vol. 1, p. 79.

9. See David Robertson, *Denmark Vesey* (1999), and Douglas R. Egerton, *He Shall Go Out Free: The Lives of Denmark Vesey* (1999).

10. Robertson, p. 123.

11. See Nell I. Painter, "Martin R. Delany: Elitism and Black Nationalism," in Leon Litwack and August Meier, eds., *Black Leaders of the Nineteenth Century* (1988).

12. Quoted in John David Smith, *Black Judas: William Hannibal Thomas and the American Negro* (2000), p. 46.

13. Ibid., p. 54.
14. Ibid., p. 45.
15. Ibid.
16. William Hannibal Thomas, *The American Negro: What He Was, What He Is, and What He May Become: A Critical and Practical Discussion* (1901), pp. 109–223, passim.
17. Ibid., p. 141.
18. Ibid., p. 162.
19. Ibid., p. 373.
20. Ibid., p. 203.
21. Quoted in Smith, p. 192.
22. Ibid., p. 193.
23. Ibid., p. 194.
24. Ibid., p. 203.
25. Charles W. Chestnutt, "A Defender of His Race," *Critic* 38.4 (April 1901), p. 350.
26. Smith, p. 299.
27. Ibid., p. 232.
28. Ibid., pp. 221, 231.
29. Judith Stein, *The World of Marcus Garvey: Race and Class in Modern Society* (1986), p. 1. See also Tony Martin, *Race First: The Ideological and Organizational Struggles of Marcus Garvey and the Universal Improvement Association* (1976); Theodore Vincent, *Black Power and the Garvey Movement* (1972); E. David Cronon, *Black Moses: The Story of Marcus Garvey and the Universal Negro Improvement Association* (1955).
30. Henry Louis Gates, Jr., and Cornel West, *The African-American Century: How Black Americans Have Shaped Our Country* (2000), p. 95.
31. Ibid.
32. *Philosophy and Opinions of Marcus Garvey*, Amy Jacques-Garvey, ed., with an introduction by Robert A. Hill (1923, 1992), vol. 1, p. 29.
33. Ibid.
34. *Philosophy and Opinions of Marcus Garvey*, vol. 2, p. 123.

35. Ibid., p. 104.
36. Ibid., p. 77.
37. Ibid., pp. 88–89.
38. Ibid., p. 59.
39. Quoted in Stephen Carter, *Reflections of an Affirmative Action Baby* (1991), p. 122.
40. *W. E. B. DuBois: A Reader,* David Levering Lewis, ed. (1995), p. 340.
41. See Theodore Kornweibel, Jr., *"Seeing Red": Federal Campaigns Against Black Military, 1919–1925* (1998), p. 112.
42. *W. E. B. DuBois: A Reader,* p. 697.
43. See Dickson D. Bruce, *Archibald Grimké: Portrait of a Black Independent* (1993), p. 222.
44. Ibid., p. 223.
45. Ibid., p. 228.
46. Quoted in Stephen R. Fox, *The Guardian of Boston: William Monroe Trotter* (1970), p. 219.
47. David Levering Lewis, *W. E. B. DuBois: Biography of a Race 1868–1919* (1993), p. 555.
48. Quoted in Chana Kai Lee, *For Freedom's Sake: The Life of Fannie Lou Hamer* (2000), p. 130.
49. Quoted in Malcolm X, "Message to the Grassroots," in *Malcolm X Speaks: Selected Speeches and Statements,* George Breitman, ed. (1965, 1990), p. 12.
50. Martin Luther King, Jr., "The Sword That Heals," *The Critic,* June–July 1964, p. 14.
51. Yasuhiro Katagiri, *The Mississippi State Sovereignty Commission: Civil Rights and States' Rights* (2001), p. 40.
52. Ibid., p. 43.
53. Ibid.
54. Ibid., p. 48.
55. Ibid., p. 49.
56. Ibid.
57. See Diane McWhorter, *Carry Me Home* (2001), p. 326.
58. See David J. Garrow, *The FBI and Martin Luther King, Jr: From "Solo" to Memphis* (1981), pp. 173–203.

59. Ibid., p. 190.

60. Kenneth O'Reilly, *"Racial Matters": The FBI's Secret File on Black America, 1960–1972* (1989), p. 268.

61. Paul Bass and Douglas W. Rae, *Murder in the Model City: The Black Panthers, Yale, and the Redemption of a Killer* (2006), p. 25.

62. See *Hampton v. Hanrahan*, 600 F.2d 600 (CA 7 1979); Robert Blau, "Panther Informant Death Ruled Suicide," *Chicago Tribune*, Jan. 18, 1990. For a dramatization of O'Neal's betrayal, see Robert Myers, *Dead of Night: The Execution of Fred Hampton* (1998).

63. See, e.g., Bass and Rae; Hugh Pearson, *The Shadow of the Panther: Huey Newton and the Price of Black Power in America* (1994).

Three THE IDEA OF THE SELLOUT IN
CONTEMPORARY BLACK AMERICA

1. John Blake, "The Soul Patrol Demanding Conformity, It Scorns Blacks Who Don't Act 'Black Enough,'" *Atlanta Journal-Constitution*, March 15, 1992.

2. Randall Robinson, *Defending the Spirit: A Black Life in America* (1998).

3. Quoted in Lynn Norment, "Black Men and White Women: What's Behind the Furor?," *Ebony*, Nov. 1994, p. 50.

4. Lawrence Otis Graham, *Member of the Club: Reflections on Life in a Racially Polarized World* (1995), p. 41.

5. Quoted in William S. McFeely, *Frederick Douglass* (1991), p. 320.

6. Jake Lamar, *Bourgeois Blues: An American Memoir* (1991), p. 156.

7. See Laura Blumenfeld, "The Nominee's Soul Mate; Clarence Thomas's Wife Shares His Ideas. She's No Stranger to Controversy. And She's Adding to His," *Washington Post*, Sept. 10, 1991.

8. See Christopher A. Darden with Jess Walter, *In Contempt* (1996), and *The Darden Dilemma: 12 Black Writers on Justice, Race, and Conflicting Loyalties,* Ellis Cose, ed. (1997).

9. Pamela Newkirk, *Within the Veil: Black Journalists, White Media* (2000), p. 147.

10. Quoted in Ibid., p. 147.

11. See Frank McCoy, "Can the Black Caucus Be Bipartisan?" *Black Enterprise,* Jan. 1994.

12. Quoted in Stephen L. Carter, *Reflections of an Affirmative Action Baby* (1991), p. 108.

13. Ibid., p. 108.

14. See, e.g., William Jelani Cobb, "The Definition of a Sellout," Africana.com, posted Nov. 30, 2004; Michael A. Fletcher, "The Linguist's Fighting Words," *Washington Post,* Jan. 3, 2001 (noting that "some have called him a sellout, a self-hater and an Uncle Tom").

15. "Condoleezza Rice: The Devil's Handmaiden," Black Commentator.com, Jan. 23, 2003.

16. Michael Eric Dyson, "I'm Gonna Get You, Sucka," Savoymag .com, Nov. 2002.

17. See, e.g., Jesse Lee Peterson, *From Rage to Responsibility: Black Conservative Jesse Lee Peterson and America Today* (2000).

18. Carter, p. 101.

19. Ibid., p. 103.

20. Glenn C. Loury, *One by One from the Inside Out: Essays and Reviews on Race and Responsibility in America* (1995), p. 190.

21. Ibid.

22. See Glen Ford and Peter Gamble, "The Hustler as Public Intellectual," BlackCommentator.com, Aug. 22, 2002.

23. Martin Kilson, "How to Spot a 'Black Trojan Horse,'" BlackCommentator.com, May 8, 2002.

24. See Kevin Mumford, *Newark: A History of Race, Rights, and Riots in America* (2007), pp. 218–23.

25. Quoted in Peter Noel, "The Uncle Tom Dilemma," *Village Voice,* Aug. 16, 2000.

26. See, e.g., Jason D. Hill, *Becoming a Cosmopolitan: What It Means to Be a Human Being in the New Millennium* (2000); Paul Gilroy, *Against Race: Imagining Political Culture Beyond the Color Line* (2000); Randall Kennedy, "My Race Problem—And Ours," *The Atlantic Monthly,* May 1997.

27. Carter, p. 139.

28. Ibid., p. 142.

29. Ibid., pp. 133, 139.

30. Ibid., p. 141.

31. Ibid., p. 195.

32. Ibid., p. 239.

33. Quoted in Lena Williams, "In a 90s Quest for Black Identity, Intense Doubts and Disagreements," *New York Times,* Nov. 30, 1991.

34. See Kimberly Jade Norwood, "The Virulence of Blackthink and How Its Threat of Ostracism Shackles Those Deemed Not Black Enough," 93 *Kentucky Law Journal* 144 (2005).

35. Carter, p. 239.

36. Randall Kennedy, "Martin Luther King's Constitution: A Legal History of the Montgomery Bus Boycott," 98 *Yale Law Journal* 999 (1989).

37. Loury, p. 191.

38. Ibid., p. 190.

Four THE CASE OF CLARENCE THOMAS

1. For biographical information on Clarence Thomas, see Kevin Merida and Michael Fletcher, *Supreme Discomfort: The Divided Soul of Clarence Thomas* (2007); Ken Foskett, *Judging Thomas: The Life and Times of Clarence Thomas* (2004); Andrew Peyton Thomas, *Clarence Thomas: A Biography* (2001); Scott Douglas Gerber, *First Principles: The Jurisprudence of Clarence Thomas* (1999); Jane Mayer and Jill

Abramson, *Strange Justice: The Selling of Clarence Thomas* (1994); Timothy M. Phelps and Helen Winternitz, *Capitol Games: Clarence Thomas, Anita Hill, and the Story of a Supreme Court Nomination* (1992).

2. Quoted in Merida and Fletcher, p. 229.

3. Barry Sanders, "No Need to Protest Thomas," *News & Observer,* March 8, 2002.

4. Senate Committee on the Judiciary, *Nomination of Judge Clarence Thomas to Be Associate Justice of the Supreme Court of the United States.* United States Congress, 1993 (hereinafter referred to as Senate Hearing), vol. 2, p. 687.

5. Quoted in Foskett, p. 329, citing *Savannah Morning News,* July 14, 2001.

6. See John Y. Odom, "Thomas Needs Memory Jog on Roots," *Wisconsin State Journal,* Aug. 23, 1998.

7. Marc Perrusquia, "Protesters Attack Thomas as a Sellout," *Commercial Appeal,* July 30, 1998.

8. See thenortheasternetwork.com/news/opinion/182027-1.html, "Justice Clarence Thomas Earns Buckwheat Award," June 24, 2003.

9. Quoted in Foskett, p. 289.

10. Quoted in Merida and Fletcher, p. 20.

11. Wiley A. Hall III, "Thomas Debate Feeds Myth: Blacks Obsessed with Race as History's Victims," *Baltimore Evening Sun,* Sept. 14, 1991.

12. Derrick Z. Jackson, "Mugging Frederick Douglass," *Boston Globe,* July 4, 2003.

13. Michael Thelwell, "False, Fleeting, Perjured Clarence: Yale's Brightest and Blackest Go to Washington," in Toni Morrison, ed., *Race-ing Justice, En-gendering Power: Essays on Anita Hill, Clarence Thomas, and the Construction of Social Reality* (1992), p. 90.

14. Quoted in Merida and Fletcher, p. 21.

15. I was directed to this polling data by an excellent unpublished paper, Kwaku A. Akownah's "Justice Thomas's Black Origi-

nalism: Conservative Advocacy, Originalist Devotion and the Turn Toward Frederick Douglass" (2004), pp. 44–45.

16. Senate Hearing, vol. 2, p. 699.

17. Ibid., p. 674.

18. Odom, "Thomas Needs Memory Jog."

19. Maureen Dowd, "Could Thomas Be Right?" *New York Times,* June 25, 2003.

20. Stephen Carter, *Reflections of an Affirmative Action Baby* (1991), p. 101. See also Deborah C. Malamud, "Values, Symbols, and Facts in the Affirmative Action Debate," 95 *Michigan Law Review* 1668, 1713 (1997). ("Affirmative action has become to the African American community what abortion rights have become for the feminist community—the constitutive issue, the program because of which we find ourselves a part of the debate rather than disempowered outsiders.")

21. Orlando Patterson, "Affirmative Action: The Sequel," *New York Times,* June 22, 2003.

22. See Christopher Edley, Jr., *Not All Black and White: Affirmative Action and American Values* (1996).

23. See Melissa Victoria Harris-Lacewell, *Barbershops, Bibles, and BET: Everyday Talk and Black Political Thought* (2004), pp. 218–27.

24. Senate Hearing, p. 846.

25. Ibid., p. 850.

26. Harris-Lacewell, p. 226. See also "Most Americans Are Undecided on Court Nomination, Poll Finds," *New York Times,* Sept. 10, 1991, quoting blacks who stated, "I think that when Thomas is positioned as a jurist, he is actually going to do the right thing. . . . He won't forget what he went through. . . . I don't care what he says publicly. He'll do the right thing . . . when the time comes."

27. Maya Angelou, "I Dare to Hope," *New York Times,* Aug. 25, 1991.

28. *Adarand Constructors, Inc. v. Pena,* 515 U.S. 200, 240 (1995).

29. Ibid., pp. 240–41.

30. *Grutter v. Bollinger,* 539 U.S. 306, 353 (2003).

31. *Adarand,* 515 U.S., 241.

32. *Grutter,* 539 U.S., 354.

33. See, e.g., Robert L. Allen, *Black Awakening in Capitalist America: An Analytic History* (1969).

34. A. Leon Higginbotham, Jr., "Justice Clarence Thomas in Retrospect," 45 *Hastings Law Journal* 1405, 1412 (1993).

35. See Juan Williams, "A Question of Fairness," *Atlantic Monthly,* Feb. 1, 1987; Diane Brady, "Online Extra: Supreme Court Justice Clarence Thomas Speaks," Businessweek.com, March 12, 2007.

36. See "Justice Clarence Thomas: A Classic Example of an Affirmative Action Baby," *Journal of Blacks in Higher Education,* Jan. 31, 1998; Angela Onwuachi-Willig, "Using the Master's 'Tool' to Dismantle the House: Why Justice Clarence Thomas Makes the Case for Affirmative Action," 47 *Arizona Law Review* 113, 115–20 (2005).

37. See Christopher Edley, Jr., "Doubting Thomas: Law, Politics and Hypocrisy," *Washington Post,* July 7, 1991; Onwuachi-Willig, pp. 116–20.

38. See Ilya Somin, "The Ethics of Benefiting from Policies That You Oppose," The Volokh Conspiracy, volokh.com, June 8, 2007.

39. See *Parents Involved in Community Schools v. Seattle School District No.1 et al.,* 127 S. Ct. 2738, 2782 (2007), (Thomas, J., concurring); *Grutter v. Bollinger,* 539 U.S. 306, 378 (2003) (Thomas, J., dissenting).

40. *Parents Involved in Community Schools,* p. 378.

41. *Plessy v. Ferguson,* 163 U.S. 537 (1896).

42. Quoted in Andrew Kull, *The Color-Blind Constitution* (1992), p. 62.

43. See Clarence Thomas, "Be Not Afraid," American Enterprise Institute, Feb. 13, 2001, found at americanradioworks.public radio.org.

44. Ibid.

45. See Samuel A. Marcosson, *Original Sin: Clarence Thomas and the Failure of the Constitutional Conservatives* (2002); Jed Rubenfeld, "Affirmative Action," 107 *Yale Law Journal* 427 (1997–1998); Eric Schnapper, "Affirmative Action and the Legislative History of the Fourteenth Amendment," 71 *Virginia Law Review* 753 (1985).

46. Rubenfeld, p. 431.

47. See Randall Kennedy, *Interracial Intimacies: Sex, Marriage, Identity, and Adoption* (2003), pp. 249–54.

48. André Douglas Pond Cummings, "*Grutter v. Bollinger,* Clarence Thomas, Affirmative Action and the Treachery of Originalism: 'The Sun Don't Shine in This Part of Town,'" 21 *Harvard BlackLetter Law Journal* 1 (2005).

49. See Owen Fiss, "Groups and the Equal Protection Clause," 5 *Philosophy & Public Affairs* 107 (1976).

50. See Robert Dahl, "Decision-making in a Democracy: The Supreme Court as a National Policy-Maker," 6 *Journal of Public Law* 279 (1957).

51. John Hart Ely, "The Constitutionality of Reverse Racial Discrimination," 41 *University of Chicago Law Review* 723 (1974).

52. See, e.g., Justice Clarence Thomas, "Civility," 39 *South Texas Law Review* 655 (1997).

53. "Civility: A Speech Delivered by Associate Justice Clarence Thomas to Students at Washington and Lee University School of Law," 4 *Race & Ethnic Ancestry Law Journal* 1 (1998).

54. *Grutter,* 539 U.S., 372, n. 11.

55. Higginbotham, p. 1426.

56. See *Hudson v. McMillan,* 503 U.S. 1 (1992).

57. William Raspberry, "Confounding One's Supporters," *Washington Post,* Feb. 28, 1992.

58. On the phase of the confirmation hearing that focused on Anita Hill's allegations, see *Race-ing Justice, En-gendering Power: Essays on Anita Hill, Clarence Thomas, and the Con-*

struction of Social Reality, Toni Morrison, ed. (1992); Timothy M. Phelps and Helen Winternitz, *Capitol Games, Race, Gender, and Power in America: The Legacy of the Hill-Thomas Hearings,* Anita Faye Hill and Emma Coleman Jordan, eds. (1995).

59. Senate Hearing, vol. 4, pp. 157–58.

60. See Emma Coleman Jordan, "The Power of False Racial Memory and the Metaphor of Lynching" in Hill and Jordan, p. 37 (Thomas's "emotional soliloquy" is widely agreed to be the point at which opinion turned in his favor"). See also John C. Danforth, *Resurrection: The Confirmation of Clarence Thomas* (1994), pp. 148–49 ("There was a general feeling among his supporters that Clarence had taken the offensive").

61. Kimberlé Crenshaw, "Whose Story Is It Anyway? Feminist and Antiracist Appropriations of Anita Hill," in *Race-ing Justice, En-gendering Power,* p. 417 ("the race ploy was amazingly successful; Thomas's approval ratings in the black community skyrocketed from 54 percent to nearly 80 percent"). See also Katheryn Russell-Brown, "Black Protectionism as a Civil Rights Strategy," 53 *Buffalo Law Review* 1 (2005).

62. Crenshaw, pp. 402–3.

63. Ibid., p. 416.

64. Ibid., p. 434.

65. Ibid.

66. Bray, *Court of Appeal,* p. 47.

67. See Orlando Patterson, "Race, Gender and Liberal Fallacies," *New York Times,* Oct. 20, 1991.

68. See Trevor Coleman, "Doubting Thomas," *Emerge,* Nov. 1993.

69. See Merida and Fletcher, pp. 222–26.

70. See John O. Calmore, "Airing Dirty Laundry: Disputes Among Privileged Blacks—From Clarence Thomas to the Law School Five," 46 *Howard Law Journal* 175 (2003).

71. Ibid., p. 225.

72. Carl Rowan, "Thomas Is Far from 'Home,'" *Chicago Sun-Times,* July 4, 1993.

73. Vincent T. Bugliosi, "None Dare Call It Treason," *Nation,* Feb. 5, 2001.

74. Quoted in Angela Onwuachi-Willig, "Just Another Brother on the SCT? What Justice Thomas Teaches Us About the Influence of Racial Identity," 90 *Iowa Law Review* 931 (2005), p. 938.

75. Ibid. See also Mark Tushnet, "Clarence Thomas's Black Nationalism," 47 *Howard Law Journal* 232 (2003).

76. *United States v. Fordice,* 505 U.S. 717 (1992) (Thomas, J., concurring).

77. Ibid., p. 745 (quoting W. E. B. DuBois, "Editorial, Schools," in *The Crisis: A Record of the Darker Races,* 1917, pp. 111–12.

78. *Fordice,* p. 749.

79. *Missouri v. Jenkins,* 515 U.S. 70, 114 (1995) (Thomas, J., concurring).

80. Ibid., pp. 121–22.

81. Ibid., p. 122.

82. *Zelman v. Simmons-Harris,* 536 U.S. 639 (2002).

83. Ibid., p. 681 (Thomas, J., concurring).

84. Ibid., pp. 682–83.

85. Quoted in Foskett, p. 276.

86. *Adarand Constructors,* 515 U.S. 243–45 (Stevens, J., dissenting).

87. See Onwuachi-Willig, "Just Another Brother," p. 938, n. 26.

88. For a critique of Rehnquist that suggests he was racist see Jerome McCristal Culp, Jr., "Understanding the Racial Discourse of Justice Rehnquist," 25 *Rutgers Law Journal* 597 (1994). For a vigorous rebuttal by some of Justice Rehnquist's law clerks (the justice never had a clerk who identified himself or herself as black), see Letter to the Editor, "62 Former Law Clerks Reject 'Outrageous Attack,'" *Legal Times,* March 15, 1993.

89. Evelyn Wilson, comments on "An Open Letter to Justice

Clarence Thomas from a Federal Judicial Colleague," 20 *Southern University Law Review* 41, 147 (1993).

90. Higginbotham, p. 1419.

91. See, e.g., Mari Matsuda, "Looking to the Bottom: Critical Legal Studies and Reparations," 22 *Harvard Civil Rights–Civil Liberties Law Review* 323 (1987).

92. See Randall Kennedy, "Racial Critiques of Legal Academia," 102 *Harvard Law Review* 1745 (1989).

93. See Michael Dawson, *Black Visions: The Roots of Contemporary African-American Political Ideologies* (2003), p. 218 (black conservatives "use the 'authenticity' derived from their own blackness to be particularly acute and visible critics of practices, values, ideologies, and leaders which they claim are damaging to the black community").

94. Calmore, p. 227.

95. Crenshaw, p. 402.

96. Higginbotham, p. 1424.

97. See Larry Gross, *Contested Closets: The Politics and Ethics of Outing* (1993), pp. 1, 28–29.

98. Ibid., pp. 3, 27.

99. See Adam Nagourney, "G.O.P. Consultant Weds His Male Partner," *New York Times,* April 9, 2005; Stephen Rodrick, "The Secret Life of Arthur J. Finkelstein," *Boston Magazine,* Oct. 1996.

Five PASSING AS SELLING OUT

1. See Randall Kennedy, *Interracial Intimacies, Sex, Marriage, Identity, and Adoption* (2003), pp. 281–338; Brooke Kroeger, *Passing: When People Can't Be Who They Are* (2003); Werner Sollors, *Neither Black Nor White Yet Both: Thematic Explorations of Interracial Literature* (1997), pp. 246–84; Louis Wirth and Herbert Goldhamer, "The Hybrid and the Problem of Miscegenation," in *Characteristics of the American Negro,* Otto Klineberg, ed. (1944).

2. St. Clair Drake and Horace R. Cayton, *Black Metropolis: A Study of Negro Life in a Northern City* (1945; reprint, 1961), p. 162.

3. See Walter White, *A Man Called White: The Autobiography of Walter White* (1948); Kenneth Robert Janken, *White: The Biography of Walter White, Mr. NAACP* (2003).

4. Janken, p. 15.

5. White, p. 136.

6. Ibid., p. 11.

7. Ibid, p. 51.

8. Lucia Stanton and Dianne Swann-Wright, "Bonds of Memory: Identity and the Hemings Family," *Sally Hemings and Thomas Jefferson: History, Memory, and Civic Culture,* in Jan Ellen Lewis and Peter S. Onuf, eds. (1999), p. 163.

9. Ibid.

10. Ibid.

11. Ibid., p. 182, n. 5.

12. Ibid., p. 164.

13. Ibid., p. 172.

14. See James M. O'Toole, *Passing: Race, Religion, and the Healy Family, 1820–1920* (2002).

15. Ibid., p. 76.

16. Ibid., p. 141.

17. Ibid., p. 90.

18. Harry A. Ploski and Roscoe C. Brown, Jr., *The Negro Almanac* (1967), p. 804. See also *The Black American Reference Book,* Mabel Smythe, ed. (1976), p. 454.

19. Quoted in Jillian A. Sim, "Fading to White," *American Heritage,* March 1999.

20. The most useful current edition of *Black No More* is the Northeastern University Press edition (1987), which offers an illuminating introduction by James A. Miller. My references are to this edition.

21. Ibid., pp. 85–86.

22. Ibid., p. 87.

23. Frances E. W. Harper, "Iola Leroy," in *The African American Novel in the Age of Reaction: Three Classics,* William L. Andrews, ed. (1992), p. 86.

24. Ibid., p. 88.

25. Ibid., pp. 177–78.

26. Ibid., p. 96.

27. Ibid., p. 97.

28. Ibid.

29. Ibid., p. 179.

30. Ibid., p. 204.

31. Ibid.

32. Nella Larsen, *Passing* (1929; reprint edited and with an introduction by Deborah E. McDowell, 1986), pp. 185–86.

33. Jessie Redmon Fauset, *Plum Bun: A Novel Without a Moral* (1928; reprint 1990), p. 15.

34. Ibid.

35. Ray Stannard Baker, *Following the Color Line: American Negro Citizenship in the Progressive Era* (1908; reprint, 1964), pp. 162–63.

36. See, e.g., Langston Hughes, "Jokes on Our White Folks," in *Langston Hughes and the Chicago Defender: Essays on Race, Politics, and Culture, 1942–62,* Christopher C. DeSantis, ed. (1995); Langston Hughes, "Fooling Our White Folks," *Negro Digest,* April 1950.

37. Gregory Howard Williams, *Life on the Color Line: The True Story of a White Boy Who Discovered He Was Black* (1995), p. 174.

38. Shirlee Taylor Haizlip, *The Sweeter the Juice* (1994), p. 64.

39. Cheryl I. Harris, "Whiteness as Property," 106 *Harvard Law Review* 1707, 1711 (1993).

40. Haizlip, p. 63.

41. Glenn C. Loury, *One by One from the Inside Out: Essays and Reviews on Race and Responsibility in America* (1995), p. 2.

42. See *Hurd v. Hodge,* 334 U.S. 24, 27, n. 2 (1948); Clement

Vose, *Caucasians Only: The Supreme Court, the NAACP, and the Restrictive Covenant Cases* (1959), pp. 85–86.

43. Leo Spitzer, *Lives in Between: The Experience of Marginality in a Century of Emancipation* (1999), p. 180.

44. Charles W. Chesnutt, *The House Behind the Cedars* (1900, 1993), p. 12.

45. Ibid., p. 20.

46. Ronald Hall, "Blacks Who Pass," in *Brotherman: The Odyssey of Black Men in America—An Anthology,* Herb Boyd and Robert L. Allen, eds. (1995), p. 475.

47. Adrian Piper, "Passing for White, Passing for Black," in *Out of Order, Out of Sight, vol. 1: Selected Essays in Meta-Art 1968–1992* (1996).

Epilogue

1. See Randall Kennedy, "On Cussing Out White Liberals," *The Nation,* Sept. 4, 1982. See also Jack Greenberg, *Crusaders in the Courts: Legal Battles of the Civil Rights Movement* (anniversary edition, 2004), pp. 542–45; Christopher Edley, Jr., "The Boycott at Harvard: Should Teaching Be Colorblind?," *Washington Post,* Aug. 18, 1982.

2. See Randall Kennedy, "Racial Critiques of Legal Academia," 102 *Harvard Law Review* 1745 (1989).

3. See Robert Williams, "Parable, Critical Race Theory Newsletter," Oct. 27, 1989, excerpted in Scott Brewer, "Introduction: Choosing Sides in the Racial Critiques Debate," 103 *Harvard Law Review* 1844, 1846 (1990); Ronald S. Roberts, *Clarence Thomas and the Tough Love Crowd: Counterfeit Heroes and Unhappy Truths* (1995), pp. 53–54; Jon Wiener, "Law Profs Fight the Power (Minority Legal Scholars)," *The Nation,* Sept. 4, 1989.

4. Martin Kilson, "Randall Kennedy's Idiotic Assault on Black People's Honor," BlackCommentator.com, June 27, 2002.

5. Glen Ford and Peter Gamble, "The Hustler as Public Intellectual," BlackCommentator.com, Aug. 22, 2002.

6. Margaret Kimberly, "Randall Kennedy Defends Racist Violence," BlackCommentator.com, June 15, 2006.

7. See Genna Rae McNeil, *Groundwork: Charles Hamilton Houston and the Struggle for Civil Rights* (1983), pp. 84, 267, n. 48.

8. See *The American Directory of Certified Uncle Toms* (2002), pp. 209–12.

Index